30 WEEKEND WALKS

London

ILLUSTRATED BY
Lucy Davey

pocket mountains

The author and publisher have made every effort to ensure that the information in this publication is accurate, and accept no responsibility whatsoever for any loss, injury or inconvenience experienced by any person or persons whilst using this book

For Colin – a great friend and unfailing font of local knowledge, who has pointed me towards more of London's curious corners and hidden treasures than I could possibly include in one book. Cheers mate, PK

published by
pocket mountains ltd
The Old Church, Moffat,
Dumfries & Galloway DG10 9HB
www.pocketmountains.com

ISBN: 978-1-907025-89-1

Printed in Glasgow by J Thomson Colour Printers Ltd.

MIX
Paper | Supporting
responsible forestry
FSC® C023105

Introduction

Once the world's biggest city, and still Western Europe's largest metropolis, London remains one of the continent's greenest capitals, with more than 3000 parks, gardens, woods, wetlands, commons, heaths, nature reserves and leafy retreats punctuating the streets, belying its concrete jungle reputation. And for all the Big Smoke's undeniable hubbub, it's easy to escape the hustle, bustle, tarmac and tumult by exploring these hidden harbours of tranquillity, which range from epic parks to tiny unexpected urban oases, often linked by canal towpaths, tree-fringed footpaths, riverbank trails and waymarked walking routes.

Wildlife thrives in these verdant environments, and the city is home to hedgehogs, deer, badgers, foxes, squirrels, water voles, stoats, multiple species of bat, butterflies, moths and dragonflies. London is also one of Earth's largest urban forests, with an estimated eight million trees inhabited by more than 300 bird species, who sing the sun up over the skyscrapers each morning. Permanent residents range from skylarks, robins, goldfinches, chiffchaffs, redwings and wood pigeons to kingfishers, kestrels and falcons. Rowdy ring-necked parakeets are new arrivals, while seasonal visitors include a wealth of waterfowl.

More than 2000 years of human habitation has shaped London's landscape, and strolling the streets permits a peek into the capital's captivating past. Besides monuments to familiar figures, you'll find touching tributes to less-famous heroes and maltreated misfortunates in places like Postman's Park and the Cross Bones Graveyard. Look out too for London's blue plaques, which celebrate the city's incredible cast of actors, artists, writers, philosophers, politicians, musicians and sporting titans.

Home to more than nine million people, and destination of choice for 30 million annual visitors, Greater London covers 1500 sq km of the Thames Valley, an area once blanketed in forest and thinly populated by Bronze Age tribes. The first sizeable settlement was founded by the Romans in 47AD. Four years after

3

the imperious Italians invaded, a trading port called Londinium was built on a bridgeable part of the river, near present-day London Bridge, where there's been a crossing ever since. Camulodunum (Colchester) was the original capital of Britannia (Roman Britain), but after Queen Boudica's warriors destroyed both cities during the ill-fated Iceni rebellion in 60–61AD, Londinium was rebuilt and rapidly grew. Within a century it was Britannia's busiest trading centre, and by around 200 a wall protected the burgeoning base. The modern City of London (the 'Square Mile') lies within the Roman wall, sections of which still stand. The city survived attacks by Saxon pirates, but the Romans left Britain in 410, and Londinium wilted.

Anglo-Saxons soon established competing kingdoms, with London passing from the Middle Saxons (whose turf became Middlesex) to the East Saxons (Essex) before being swallowed by Mercia. Weirdly, they ignored the old walled city, but remains of an Anglo-Saxon cemetery have been unearthed at Covent Garden, along with evidence of habitation around Trafalgar Square. Christianity caught on in the 7th century, and the original St Paul's was built in 604 (close to the current cathedral).

Vikings sacked the city twice in the 9th century, and in 871 the Great Heathen Army occupied London. The 'Danelaw' covered most of the country until Alfred the Great of Wessex and his sons vanquished the Vikings and created the Kingdom of England. Winchester was the capital, but London grew anew. King Athelstan convened his Witan ('council of wise men') here, and Æthelred the Unready issued the Laws of London in 978. The Vikings returned with a vengeance in 1013; Sweyn Forkbeard's forces overran the country and his son, Cnut the Great, became king of England, Denmark and Norway. When Anglo-Saxon rule resumed in 1042, Edward the Confessor founded Westminster Abbey, where his successor, Harold Godwinson, was crowned in 1066. Ten months later, however, Harold was defeated and killed at the Battle of Hastings.

The Norman newcomers firmly established London as England's capital. William the Conqueror was crowned in

Westminster Abbey and by 1078 he had built the White Tower (the Tower of London's centrepiece). His son, William Rufus, established Westminster Hall, which survives in the Palace of Westminster, still Britain's seat of government – a place of increasing importance after King John conceded some of the monarch's absolute authority by signing the *Magna Carta* by the Thames at Runnymede in 1215.

The Black Death halved the population in the 14th century, but London soon became one of Europe's most important economic centres, with the powerful Company of Merchant Adventurers of London launching in 1407.

During the Reformation and Henry VIII's Dissolution of the Monasteries in the 1530s, swathes of church land were seized and redistributed between the king and his cronies. Many of London's largest green spaces – including Greenwich, Richmond, Hyde and Bushy Parks – became exclusive royal hunting grounds, and the later Enclosure Acts increasingly expelled ordinary people from the commonland that once sustained them.

Culturally, London blossomed during the English Renaissance under Elizabeth I with Shakespeare staging popular plays in theatres like The Globe, now faithfully recreated on South Bank. By the Union of the Crowns in 1603, when the coronation of James VI of Scotland as King James I of England and Ireland nominally united the British Isles, the capital's population approached 225,000. London's largest public square, Lincoln's Inn Fields, opened in 1629, and Covent Garden was created soon after. The West End attracted aristocrats under Charles I, but the monarch's quarrels with his powerful parliament resulted in the eruption of the English Civil War in 1642. London largely sided with Cromwell's New Model Army, and on 30 January 1649, Charles was beheaded outside Banqueting House, now the sole surviving part of the Palace of Whitehall.

During the Interregnum period, po-faced Puritans banned theatre (along with Christmas and Easter festivities), but the arts flourished again after the Restoration in 1660. London was devastated by the Great Plague in 1665 and scorched by the Great Fire in 1666, but from the ashes the city was reborn. Christopher Wren sculpted the skyline from scratch, orchestrating the construction of St Paul's Cathedral among many other buildings. The Royal Observatory was established in Greenwich, Piccadilly became popular with the wealthy and better building materials were used throughout.

After James II was deposed in the Glorious Revolution (1688–89), the new Dutch king, William III, expanded London's boundaries by relocating the royal residence to Kensington, where it remained until George III bought Buckingham House. The 1707 Act of Union merged the Scottish and English Parliaments (with the Acts of Union 1800 adding Ireland), making London the capital of the United Kingdom, the epicentre of the expanding British Empire and the principal beneficiary of the dawning Industrial Revolution.

For centuries London Bridge was the only central structure spanning the Thames, but in 1729 a temporary bridge was built in Putney, followed by Westminster Bridge (1750), Kew Bridge (1759), Blackfriars Bridge (1769), Battersea Bridge (1773) and Richmond Bridge (1777), creating an explosion of development along the south bank. Around 1800, London became the world's first city with a million residents, and the capital continued to swell. New arrivals included Jews and Huguenots escaping religious persecution, and Irish fleeing a terrible famine Westminster's Whig government had exacerbated with its laissez-faire policies.

Evocatively described by Dickens, 19th-century London was a place of enormous wealth discrepancy, deprivation, disease and crime, with overcrowded slums and prison barges bobbing on a poisonously polluted Thames. Dreadful sanitation led to deadly cholera and typhoid endemics until the infamous Great Stink of 1858 prompted the commissioning of an ambitious sewer system proposed, designed and delivered by civil-engineering genius Joseph Bazalgette, which saw the creation of Victoria, Chelsea and Albert Embankments. Other visionary Victorians recognised the value of verdant spaces, and several of London's finest outdoor arenas opened in this era, including Victoria Park, Finsbury Park and Primrose Hill. Over the next century, the public regained access to land long-held privately by privileged families, through benevolent donation (Waterlow Park), because it was purchased by local authorities (Highgate and Queen's Woods, Holland Park), adopted by charities like the National Trust and London Wildlife Trust (Petts Wood, Sydenham Hill Wood), or fought for by community groups (Hampstead Heath, Epping Forest). The arrival of the railway in the 1830s and the London Underground (1863) further reshaped the city, enabling the mushrooming middle classes to decamp to leafy suburbs and commute to work.

London experienced Zeppelin air raids during WWI, but greater horror was unleashed by the Luftwaffe in WWII. Entire areas were bombed to oblivion during the Blitz, especially in the East End, where working-class residents had resolutely repelled the rise of British fascism between the wars. The shell-shocked population rebuilt the city, assisted by newcomers, including the Windrush generation from the Caribbean, who – despite facing discrimination on arrival (and, scandalously, official mistreatment more recently) – helped transform London into a modern multicultural metropolis, where you can find cuisine from every corner of the world and enjoy the culture and company of people from all over the planet. The city remains a progressive font of fashion, art and innovative ideas.

This guide explores Central and Greater London via 30 walks within the M25, encountering echoes of all these events. While some routes are relatively long, options always exist for shortening or dividing them into easier strolls. London's transport system is excellent and highly interconnected; you're never far from a tube or train station, bus stop or river pier, which will soon send you towards wherever you'd like to go within the capital, the country or the continent.

Contents

1

The South Bank and Bankside

Distance 3km **Time** 1 hour 30
Start Waterloo ⊖ ≋
Finish London Bridge ⊖ ≋

Tracing the tidal Thames along the South Bank and Bankside, this relatively short riverside ramble passes some of London's best-known buildings and explores the places where several of the capital's most influential inhabitants lived and worked as they shaped the city's skyline and the country's culture, amid the brothels and bars this bank was once renowned for.

From the crowded concourse of Waterloo, Britain's busiest railway station, head past Platform 19 towards the main entrance/exit, pausing to contemplate the poignant National Windrush Monument, created by Jamaican artist Basil Watson. Unveiled in 2022, the brass sculpture depicts a newly arrived family, representatives of a generation of Caribbean people who began disembarking from trains here in the late 1940s in response to an invitation from the British government (reeling from a severe labour shortage) to come and help rebuild London after WWII.

Leave the station via the steps and glance back to view Victory Arch, built after WWI, which bears the names of the many railway staff killed in the conflict. Turn left on Cab Road and cross busy York Road at the lights. Continue straight ahead along pedestrianised Sutton Walk as it sneaks beneath railway tracks and, when you reach Concert Hall Approach, turn left. Pass White House Gardens on your right and cross Belvedere Road to reach Royal Festival Hall. From Friday to Sunday, the fantastic and aromatic Southbank Centre Food Market here offers all sorts of sensational cuisine from around the world, as well as excellent coffee and sweet treats.

Continue up the steps beside the Southbank Centre, Europe's largest art and performance space, passing a bust of anti-Apartheid freedom fighter and

11

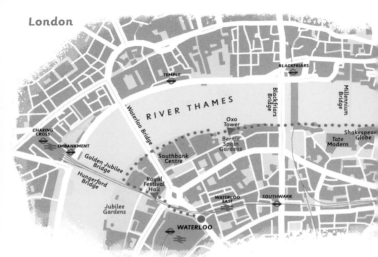

former president of South Africa, Nelson Mandela. This – the second version of the sculpture, commissioned after the first was destroyed by right-wing protesters – was unveiled by the Greater London Council (GLC) in 1988, two years before Mandela was released from jail and 25 years ahead of his death (a rare break with the tradition of not honouring people in statue form during their lifetime).

Ahead, Hungerford Bridge takes trains across the broad Thames, while pedestrians cross the river on the Golden Jubilee Bridge, running parallel to the railway. However, this route

turns right and descends steps to walk east along the South Bank. Pass Festival Pier on your left and watch the aerial antics of skateboarders in the graffiti-garnished undercroft below the concrete shell of Queen Elizabeth Hall.

Continue past the BFI (British Film Institute) to Waterloo Bridge, beneath which an excellent open-air book market has been beguiling bibliophiles daily since 1983. Nearby, an effigy of Laurence Olivier strikes a thespian pose outside the National Theatre, which the performer helped establish and where he became director.

The next section would have been

of the city forming a backdrop, before the next tide washes in and wipes the canvas clean.

On the right as you round the corner are the chic boutiques, art parlours and international eateries of Gabriel's Wharf. Opposite Gabriel's Pier, Bernie Spain Gardens supply breathing space between the buildings. This green area is named after Bernadette Spain, a resident who successfully led the resistance against brutal office developments planned here in the 1970s, which would have cut off public access to the riverside.

Walk around, or enter and explore, Oxo Tower Wharf – a design hub housed within one of the South Bank's most iconic buildings, saved from demolition and development in the 1980s by the GLC and Coin Street Community Builders. At ground level find cafés and shops, while the second and third floors are occupied by artisans creating and selling all sorts of amazing stuff. At the top of the tower the rooftop gardens of OXO Tower Restaurant, Brasserie and Bar offer fabulous views across the river.

buried beneath the ill-fated Garden Bridge, had the whole project not collapsed under a heap of egos and opprobrium, but fortunately you can still stroll for free along the broad boulevard, beneath long-standing London plane trees, enjoying views across the water to white-liveried HMS *Wellington*, Britain's last surviving WWII warship from the Battle of the Atlantic.

When the path wends right, look over the railings directly ahead to the cove below. Here, when the water is low, skilled sand sculptors create incredibly detailed but ephemeral works of art on the exposed beach, with the buildings

Go past the Curzon Sea Containers hotel and cinema, and walk through a tiled tunnel beneath Blackfriars Bridge, which spans the Thames at the point where the River Fleet joins the flow (from the north bank). Mosaics detail the design and history of the current structure, which opened in 1869, replacing the original bridge built a century earlier.

Continue beneath the arches of Blackfriars Railway Bridge and station, which extends out over the river, to a section of the riverfront known as Bankside. Just past the Founder's Arms are the gardens in front of the Tate Modern. The riverside area outside the free-to-enter gallery, where the UK's collection of international modern and contemporary art is housed in a former power station, typically teems with tourists watching the antics of street performers.

Just beyond the steel supports of the Millennium Footbridge, opposite St Paul's, is Cardinals Wharf, where Christopher Wren lived while watching his magnum opus take shape (although the blue plaque on No 49, not built until 1710, is a little misleading). Virtually next door is Shakespeare's Globe, a faithful recreation of the Elizabethan-era Globe Theatre where the Bard staged (and acted in) his many plays, built 230m from where the original stood until it burnt down in 1613. Just past Bankside Pier, a few metres into Bear Gardens (named after the Davies Amphitheatre, London's last legal bear-baiting pit) is Ferryman's Seat, where the boatmen who took travellers across the Thames would rest between rides.

Go through the arch beneath Southwark Bridge. By the Anchor, turn right along Bankend, then left along the cobbles of Clink Street, walking through arches to a touristic museum on the site of the old prison. Dating to 1144, The Clink was one of London's oldest and most notorious jails – for six centuries it was a place of detention for the unruly, the unfortunate and the uncowed, with people imprisoned for offences ranging from drunkenness and debt to religious dissent and heresy. The name, now a widely used slang term for all prisons, long outlived the institution, which was razed by rioters in 1780.

The Clink was owned by the Bishop of Winchester (who also licensed the local prostitutes, known in medieval times as 'Winchester Geese') and just beyond the prison site lie the ruined remains of 13th-century Winchester Palace, the Bishops' historic London residence. Clink Street segues into Pickfords Wharf, at the end of which, berthed in St Mary Overie Dock, you'll find *The Golden Hinde* – a full-size replica of the galleon launched as *The Pelican* in 1577, but renamed *The Golden Hind* by Francis Drake during his circumnavigation of the world in 1577–80. From the front of the ship, follow Cathedral Street to the imposing Gothic edifice of Southwark

Cathedral, occupying a spot where a church has stood for more than 1000 years. The oldest elements of the current cathedral date to 1220.

To your right is bustling Borough Market, which has been operating in some form since the 12th century and now serves up gorgeous grub from all over the world from Tuesday to Sunday. This is the perfect place to pause for a pint or something to eat.

Cathedral Street ultimately spits you out onto busy Borough High Street, where an entrance to London Bridge tube is directly opposite. Before you go, though, there's much to explore around London Bridge, including the occasionally macabre but truly fascinating Old Operating Theatre Museum, where in the 1960s a complete 19th-century operating theatre with viewing seats was discovered in a boarded-up attic of the old St Thomas' Hospital, offering a chilling insight into surgical procedures and patient experiences in the days before anaesthetic and antiseptic.

2

Westminster to Pimlico

Distance 5km to Pimlico
(6.25km to Victoria) **Time** 2 hours
Start Waterloo ⊖ ≥
Finish Pimlico ⊖ or Victoria ⊖ ≥

**From London's longest legal
graffiti wall to the doors of
Tate Britain, this walk meanders
past modern art and wends
through Westminster – epicentre
of power and heart of the English
establishment for more than
a millennium.**

Leave Waterloo station via Exit 1,
located beside Platform 1, and turn right
along Cab Road, following arrows for
Lower Marsh. Use the zebra crossing,
turn left down the steps directly opposite
and walk along Spur Road. At the
bottom, where there's another zebra
crossing, turn right and go straight along
pedestrianised Lower Marsh.

Each weekday, Lower Marsh is busy
with market stalls offering everything
from aromatic street food and cool craft
to second-hand records. Cafés, bars and
restaurants line the pavements, and this
historic spot – a market and meeting

place since the 1800s – is great for
grabbing an early bite (and a vibrant
location to return to after dark, when
there's often live music and film
screenings). Keep walking, passing
Johanna Street on the left and crossing
the intersection of Launcelot and
Frazier Streets.

Go past Grindal Street on your left and
then turn right at Leake Street,
descending the walkway to enter Leake
Street Arches, where you'll be met with
the smell of spray paint and an explosion
of colour and creativity. A long tunnel
comprised of eight railway arches, this
extraordinary underpass is an ever-
changing exhibition of graffiti, often
featuring work by leading street artists
(including Blek le Rat). There are several
buzzing bars, cafés and restaurants
beneath street level here too, many of
which host live entertainment, including
comedy, theatre and music. You can
even do artist-led graffiti workshops.

Exit the arches and continue straight
ahead to busy York Road. Cross at the
lights and go up Chicheley Street,
towards the unmissable London Eye.

London

Cross Belvedere Road and walk through throngs of tourists to the base of the Millennium Wheel – Britain's most popular paid attraction – which spins slowly above Jubilee Gardens on the South Bank, right on the edge of the Thames. Across the river, a gilded eagle appears to be about to take flight – this is a monument to Royal Air Force servicemen killed in WWI.

Turn left along the river and walk in the direction of the Palace of Westminster, home to the Houses of Parliament and Big Ben (as the Great Clock of Westminster is popularly known, although the nickname specifically refers to the big bell within the tall tower), which dominates the opposite bank. Pass the London Dungeon and Sea Life London Aquarium, and continue under Westminster Bridge before immediately turning left and climbing the steps to ascend the bridge. Cross the broad Thames across Westminster Bridge, walking directly towards Westminster.

On the north bank, continue along Bridge Street into Parliament Square, looking left through the ironwork to see the extraordinary detail in the sculptured

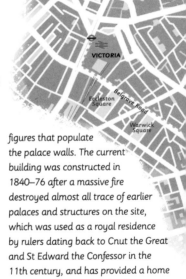

figures that populate the palace walls. The current building was constructed in 1840–76 after a massive fire destroyed almost all trace of earlier palaces and structures on the site, which was used as a royal residence by rulers dating back to Cnut the Great and St Edward the Confessor in the 11th century, and has provided a home for the Parliament of England since its inception in the 13th century.

When you see stony faced Winston Churchill frowning down at you, turn left

where 40 English monarchs have had crowns placed on their heads, starting with the last Anglo-Saxon king, ill-fated Harold II, in January 1066 (shortly followed by William the Conqueror on Christmas Day that same year). The existing Gothic church was begun under Henry III in 1245, and contains the remains of thousands of the country's luminaries, from kings and queens to politicians, scientists, soldiers and writers.

Continue past Cromwell Green and statues of Oliver Cromwell and Richard the Lionheart on your left, and an effigy of George V on your right. Just beyond the 14th-century Jewel Tower (on the right), turn left to enter Victoria Tower Gardens South. Pass a statue of political activist and leading suffragette Emmeline Pankhurst and go through the park towards the Thames, passing Auguste Rodin's *Burghers of Calais*, which

along the side of Parliament Square and then continue along St Margaret Street, walking with Westminster Abbey on your right and the Houses of Parliament on your left. The abbey occupies a spot

19

commemorates France's surrender of Calais to the English in 1347, after a long siege during the Hundred Years' War.

Turn right and walk along the riverside with the water on your left. Pass the Buxton Memorial Fountain, which celebrates the fight for abolition and the emancipation of slaves across the British Empire in 1834, and Horseferry children's playground (where there are public toilets), and continue to Lambeth Bridge. Use the zebra crossing, but stay on the north bank of the river and continue through Victoria Tower Gardens with Thames House, HQ of Britain's domestic intelligence service (MI5), on your right. Exit the gardens onto Millbank and keep walking in the same direction, past Millbank Tower and the Millbank Millennium Pier (from where you can catch a boat back towards Waterloo).

Soon you will pass Tate Britain on your right. Formerly the National Gallery of British Art, this fantastic free-to-enter gallery is home to a massive collection of modern and contemporary art, including works by Francis Bacon, William Blake, Thomas Gainsborough, John Constable, J M W Turner, Anna Lea Merritt, Pablo Picasso, Bridget Riley, Tracey Emin, Kudzanai-Violet Hwami, Lydia Ourahmane and many more.

Continue towards Vauxhall Bridge, turning left when the walkway steers away from the road opposite *Jeté* (a statue of the ballet dancer David Wall by Enzo Plazzotta) into Riverside Walk Gardens. Note the round buttress marking the site where Millbank Prison stood from 1816 to 1890; from here, convicts being transported to Australia were loaded on barges to start their long journey. Pass *Locking Piece*, a sculpture by Henry Moore, and the stunning work *Khadine* by Bruno Catalano. On the opposite side of the river, spy the multi-tiered cream-coloured building on Albert Embankment: home to the UK's foreign intelligence agency, the Secret Intelligence Service (MI6)...shhhh!

Meeting Vauxhall Bridge, go up some steps and turn right briefly to cross the road at traffic lights. Turn left and return to the Thames, descending steps and walking along the riverside path, through the gates of Crown Reach. Emerge and follow a fingerpost pointing along Grosvenor Road and the Thames Path towards Chelsea Bridge. Duck immediately left again, back to the riverside, and pass a plaque about the River Tyburn engraved by Paul Mason, close to where one channel of the hidden Tyburn joins the Thames.

Continue until you emerge into the serene surrounds of Pimlico Gardens. Go past the statue of William Huskisson (an MP with the dubious distinction of being the first person to get run over and killed by a train, after he was hit by Robert Stephenson's pioneering locomotive *The Rocket* in 1828). Carry on through the little park to *The Helmsman* (a sculpture by André Wallace), before exiting the gates and crossing Grosvenor Road.

Walk up St George's Square, going through gates and exploring the wide green central garden strip, full of benches, with elegant Georgian terraces on either side. Exit the gardens via a gate on your left, opposite a fountain in the midst of a grassy oval, then go right and walk past St Saviour's Church. Turn right on Lupus Street and Pimlico Station is 100m ahead.

Alternatively, cross Lupus Street from St Saviour's Church to carry on past the little triangular extension of St George's Square onto Belgrave Road, passing Warwick Square and Eccleston Square as you make your way to Victoria Station.

3

Soho to St Paul's

Distance 6km **Time** 2 hours
Start Oxford Circus ⊖
Finish St Paul's ⊖

A trail of two cities, this trek tiptoes from the outrageously boho streets of Soho, through kaleidoscopically colourful Chinatown and London's glitzy Theatreland, to the contemplative surrounds of Postman's Park and St Paul's Cathedral. It's not a long walk, but it is an exercise in exploration – diving into the cheek-by-jowl juxtaposition of vice and self-sacrifice, hedonism and heroism found deep in London's vibrant midst.

Leave Oxford Circus tube using Exit 6 and turn left along Argyll Street. Pass the London Palladium and go left along Great Marlborough Street, opposite Liberty. Turn right into Carnaby Street, a pedestrianised boulevard lined with boutique stores and synonymous with male fashion since the 1950s when sartorial visionaries such as John 'King of Carnaby Street' Stephen set up shop selling men's clothes wildly different to anything else available. From the Swinging Sixties onwards, Carnaby Street has energised endless era-defining cultural and musical movements, from mods, punks and skins to the New Romantics. More mainstream now than in its flamboyant heyday, it still attracts plenty of characters, artists, innovators and oddballs.

Continue past Foubert's Place and Ganton Street. At the junction with Broadwick Street, look left to see Julian Opie's *Shaida Walking*, a very modern moving artwork, and *The Spirit of Soho*, a towering mural collectively created by the community in 1991. According to some, the name 'Soho' derives from a hunting call that would have been heard when it was all fields around here; there's no hard evidence to support this theory, but the mural visually references it, with the inclusion of a hare riding a hunting dog.

At the T-junction with Beak Street, glance right to see an iconic 'Soho' sign straddling the street, but turn left. Go left again on Lexington Street, then right on

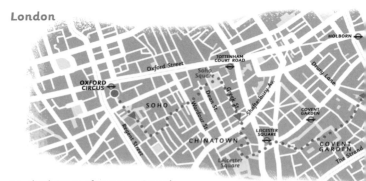

Broadwick Street. After crossing Berwick Street (where a food market offers great global grub from Monday to Saturday) and passing the Blue Posts, dogleg across Wardour Street (left, then right) to go along St Anne's Court, where David Bowie recorded his *Hunky Dory*, *The Rise and Fall of Ziggy Stardust and the Spiders from Mars* and *Space Oddity* albums in Trident Studios.

Turn left on Dean Street, then right along Carlisle Street to reach Soho Square, a little oasis of verdant peace amongst the madness, where if you're lucky you'll find a free bench. One seat, dedicated to the memory of Kirsty MacColl, is inscribed with pertinent words from one of the much-missed artist's songs: 'One day I'll be waiting there, no empty bench in Soho Square'. Walk past the mock-Tudor gazebo, exit

the square and turn right. Pass the historic House of St Barnabas, featuring the tiled words 'House of Charity' – once occupied by Joseph Bazalgette (who built London's ingenious sewer network) and later used by charities and a philanthropic club with many celebrity members and a long tradition of offering refuge to the homeless and needy. Continue south along Greek Street, past lots of lively little bars with big backstories, including Jazz After Dark where Amy Winehouse began her career.

Cross Old Compton Street by Prince Edward Theatre and The Three Greyhounds and go past (or, better still, go in) the legendary Coach and Horses on the corner of Romilly Street. This Soho supping stop may look basic but it became famous for having London's

rudest landlord and being favoured and
frequented by libation-loving literary
types ranging from Jeffrey Bernard to
Private Eye staff, who regularly held
editorial meetings here.

Emerge on Shaftesbury Avenue by
the Palace Theatre, cross using the traffic
island, turn right and then immediately
left along Gerrard Place into the chaos
and colour of Chinatown. Bear left and
go straight along Newport Place and
then right along Lisle Street, across from
the Hippodrome, before turning left
along Leicester Place to Leicester Square.
Although the Shakespeare Fountain and
Statue occupies centre stage, Leicester
Square is the heart of London's cinema
scene. Major film premieres happen here,
and it is populated by statues of celluloid

heroes ranging from Charlie Chaplin
to Mary Poppins, Bugs Bunny and
Paddington Bear.

Turn left and walk along Cranbourn
Street, past the front of the Hippodrome,
heading towards Leicester Square tube.
You're in Theatreland proper now. Cross
Charing Cross Road at the lights and
continue along Cranbourn Street. Cross
St Martins Lane, then go slightly right
along Garrick Street, before ducking left
on King Street to enter Covent Garden.
Meander around the pedestrianised
piazza, home to the Royal Opera House,
enjoying street performances by 17th-
century St Paul's Church and resisting
(or succumbing to) myriad tasty
temptations in the food, craft and retail
outlets surrounding the Apple Market.

Leave along Russell Street, go over Wellington Street at the zebra crossing and continue past the Theatre Royal Drury Lane, on your right. Cross Drury Lane and go straight along Kemble Street. Turn left on Kingsway to cross at the lights, then go right briefly until you're almost opposite Kemble Street, before strolling up Sardinia Street to Lincoln's Inn Fields. Bear left by the tennis courts, then go right and walk through the middle of the green square where squirrels scamper among sycamores. Surrounded by courts and legal institutions, London's largest public square was once the scene of several high-profile executions, including the gorily botched beheading of Lord William Russell in 1683.

Leave via the middle gate, opposite Lincoln's Inn itself, and turn right. Continue along Serle Street, before turning left on Carey Street opposite the grand National Justice Museum. After the Seven Stars, turn right on Chancery Lane by King's College London Maughan Library. Walk to the T-junction, where The Strand segues into Fleet Street on one of London's oldest thoroughfares, in constant use since the Middle Ages. To the right are the Royal Courts of Justice and St Clement Danes Church, but this route turns left along Fleet Street, a place latterly famous for its association with newspapers, but where printing has been happening for five centuries.

Divert left along Bolt Court to see the house of Dr Samuel Johnson, the 18th-century writer and lexicographer best known for compiling the first definitive English dictionary. Signs deliver you to the door of Dr Johnson's House at 17 Gough Square, a 300-year-old townhouse you can pay to enter. Pass a statue of Johnson's beloved cat, Hodge, and venture into Gunpowder Square, before turning right on Wine Office Court to return to Fleet Street, passing Ye Olde Cheshire Cheese on the corner. Rebuilt in 1667 on the site of a tale-drenched drinking den, this is one of several sensational historic pubs along Fleet Street.

Continue over Shoe Lane and Poppins Court, before crossing Farringdon Street at Ludgate Circus, where the now-subterranean River Fleet runs in darkness beneath your feet. Climb Ludgate Hill towards the instantly recognisable dome of St Paul's Cathedral, which crowns the City of London's highest point and was London's tallest building for 250 years. The current cathedral was completed in 1710 (replacing an ancient church that dated to 604AD) to the design of the peerless London skyline-sculptor Christopher Wren.

Cross Limeburner Lane and turn left along Old Bailey, a street that traces the foundations of an ancient wall built to defend London in Roman times. Pass the famous criminal court, where England's most notorious lawbreakers have been sentenced since medieval times, and turn right on Newgate Street, site of the old Newgate Prison. Until 1868, public hangings were conducted outside the Old Bailey, with the condemned being paraded along Deadman's Walk between the prison and the court.

After Christchurch Greyfriars Church, site of an old monastery, turn left along Greyfriars

Passage and left again on King Edward Street. Pass a statue of Rowland Hill (social reformer, post-service pioneer and inventor of the postage stamp) to the corner of Little Britain (yes, really) by Britain's oldest functioning hospital, St Bartholomew's, founded in 1123.

Cross the road and enter Postman's Park, a large but understated pocket of peace where, in 1900, Victorian artist George Frederick Watts established a memorial wall to celebrate acts of extraordinary heroism by very ordinary people, including children, who lost their lives while saving others. The stories detailed on the Watts Memorial to Heroic Self-Sacrifice are incredibly poignant, and it's well worth reading them. Afterwards, leave the park via St Martin's Le Grand, turn right and make your way towards St Paul's Cathedral and tube station.

HODGE

Marshalsea to Wapping

Distance 6km **Time** 2 hours 30
Start Borough ⊖
Finish Wapping ⊖

This captivating walk from the site of Marshalsea Prison to Execution Dock traces the final route traditionally taken by those convicted of capital offences by the Admiralty Courts.

For four centuries, until as recently as 1830, condemned pirates, smugglers, mutineers and people found guilty of murder at sea were paraded through the streets of Borough, taken over London Bridge and past The Tower to be hanged on the banks of the Thames in Wapping, where they were left dangling until three tides had washed over them. This route also explores the evocative Cross Bones Graveyard, visits the spot where the Great Fire of London began and attends an ancient open-air church where a congregation of trees reaches for the heavens amid a crowd of traders and their cloud-scraping concrete temples.

Exit Borough tube station, turn left and go across Marshalsea Road. Cross Borough High Street at the lights, walking towards St George the Martyr, and turn left. Just past the church, hook right into Tabard Street, where every weekday a vibrant food market offers international street cuisine.

After about 50m, duck left into St George's Churchyard Gardens. Walk through the little green, looking for a plaque about Marshalsea Prison on the stone wall to your left. This wall is the only surviving part of the jail, which was originally built in 1373, shut in 1842 and was mostly demolished in the 1870s. Besides housing maritime miscreants, Marshalsea was also used to imprison debtors, including the father of Charles Dickens, and the author later depicted the horrors of the jail in works including *Little Dorrit*.

Go through a gate, turn left and walk along an alley where engraved paving stones reveal the backstory to *Little Dorrit* and excerpts from the book appear on the wall. Exit onto Borough High Street and turn right, where you'll see the John Harvard Library, named after a local man who sailed to Massachusetts in

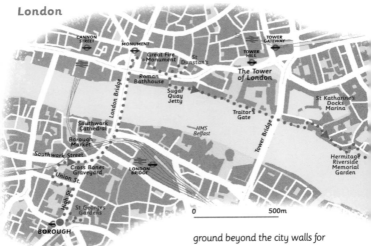

1637 and later helped found Harvard University. Continue along Borough High Street, walking north towards the Shard, stabbing at the sky in the near distance.

Pass Mermaid Court and cross Borough High Street at the lights just before Newcomen Street. Turn left along Union Street and, after about 100m, you'll reach the Cross Bones Graveyard on your right. This poignant garden of remembrance commemorates the 'outcast dead', medieval London's underclass – prostitutes, paupers and alleged criminals – whose bodies were dumped in this corner of unconsecrated

ground beyond the city walls for centuries. Contemplate the memorial to the 'Winchester Geese', local prostitutes licensed by the Bishops of Winchester, men who were happy to pocket profits from the women's work but refused to grant them a last resting place on hallowed ground.

Turn right along Redcross Way, go under railway arches, then head right on Southwark Street. Rejoin Borough High Street, cross at the lights and go left.

Walk past a London Bridge tube station entrance, pass Borough Market (on your left), cross Duke Street Hill at the lights and continue over London Bridge. As you look towards Tower

Bridge, across the bows of HMS *Belfast* (a battleship now permanently moored and used by the Imperial War Museum), the Shard is to your right and 20 Fenchurch Street (a building popularly known as the 'Walkie-Talkie') is left.

You can join the Thames Path straight after the bridge, but this route continues along the road, before turning right on Monument Street and strolling down to The Monument which commemorates the Great Fire of London. Continue past this Christopher Wren-designed Doric Column to Pudding Lane, where the blaze began in a baker's shop on 2 September 1666 before devastating

a large part of the capital along the north bank of the Thames.

Cross Pudding Lane and meander along Monument Street, emerging on Lower Thames Street by The Walrus & The Carpenter pub. Continue past St Mary at Hill, passing Billingsgate Roman House and Baths, then turn left on St Dunstan's Hill. Keep left, walk along Idol Lane and, at All Hallows House, turn right into St Dunstan-in-the-East. Originally built around 1100, this church was engulfed by the Great Fire of London. Christopher Wren designed a new steeple, but the building was ruined again during the Blitz in WWII. It remains roofless, but several walls still stand and oak, palm, magnolia, oleander and cherry trees now grow inside the church and around the gardens, creating a peaceful refuge for book-toting lunch-munching Londoners.

Continue through the churchyard, then turn right on St Dunstan's Hill and return to Lower Thames Street. Turn right, go back past the site of the Roman bathhouse, cross at the lights and dogleg (right, then left) to go along Old Billingsgate Walk. Emerge at the Thames opposite the Shard, turn left along a wooden walkway and stroll with the river on your right. Pass a couple of old cranes and venture out on Sugar Quay Jetty, opposite HMS *Belfast*.

The Thames Path veers away from the water at Three Quays Walk, taking you close to the modern entrance to the Tower of London, which looms large on your left. Return to the riverside, passing through gates and going past the little Middle Tower and Wharfinger Cottage. Bear left and walk between the Tower's western entrance and the Queen's Stairs, famously ascended by ill-fated Anne Boleyn both before her coronation in 1533 and her execution almost exactly three years later. Read the information boards along this section as you pass Children's Beach, St Thomas's Tower, Traitors' Gate (through which prisoners once arrived by boat) and the original White Tower, built by William the Conqueror in 1078. Beyond Cradle Tower and the East Drawbridge, you pass several cannons and go under an arch of Tower Bridge, which spans the river to your right.

Keep tracing the Thames, passing the *Girl with a Dolphin* sculpture and a huge sundial by the Tower Hotel. Cross a footbridge over the river entrance to St Katharine Docks and bear left into the massive marina, where scores of flashy yachts are moored. Turn right along St Katharine's Way and walk past Devon House, following signage for Wapping Woods and King Edward Memorial Park.

The river is obscured as you meander past President Quay and HMS President (a building). Pass Alderman Stairs (which only offer a brief glimpse of the water) and then go right, following a Thames Path arrow to emerge on Tower Bridge Wharf, where you can walk along the riverbank for 100m before the path bends left to meet St Katharine's Way again. Go right and right again on Wapping High Street, which rejoins the riverside at Hermitage Riverside Memorial Garden. Bombing during WWII completely levelled much of this area, and the Blitz Memorial here forms a dove-shaped frame through which you can view the Shard and Tower Bridge.

After skirting several residential buildings, the Thames Path emerges back on Wapping High Street at

Pier Head. According to tradition, condemned prisoners were permitted a last drink before going to the gallows, and the surviving taverns here are full of stories and atmosphere. By the fantastic Town of Ramsgate pub (which has been serving pints since the 16th century) you can go down Wapping Old Stairs to visit one possible location of Execution Dock (the exact position has been lost to time and tides).

Continue along Wapping High Street, past Pierhead Wharf and Waterside Gardens. Just beyond the Marine Police Unit HQ (home to England's oldest police force) and St John's Wharf, you'll find The Captain Kidd, another historic tavern, this one named after the Scottish privateer Captain William Kidd, who was hanged for piracy here in 1701. In a cruel custom, convicted pirates were hanged with a short rope, so instead of the drop breaking their neck they endured a slower death by asphyxiation, doing what was gruesomely known as the 'Marshal's dance' as their limbs flailed around. The unfortunate Kidd had to be hanged twice because the rope broke during the first attempt.

King Henry's Stairs, just past the pub, lead to another spot on the riverbank often claimed as the location of Execution Dock.

Wapping overground station is just 100m further along the High Street, but if you're enjoying exploring the excellent pubs along this stretch of the river, continue for another 500m and turn right along Wapping Wall to finish your walk in the Prospect of Whitby. Have a beer in the balcony bar, overlooking Wapping Beach, where a scaffold and noose stand as a macabre reminder of past events.

5

Cable Street to Canary Wharf

Distance 4km **Time** 2 hours
Start Shadwell ⊖
Finish Canary Wharf ⊖ ⊖

From the site of a famous pre-WWII battle fought between British fascists and defiant Eastenders, this walk wanders through leafy parks and along quiet canals and riverside paths linking the former factories, docks and wharfs of this once heavily industrialised area – close to where the 'Jack the Ripper' murders took place in 1888 – to culminate at Canary Wharf on the Isle of Dogs, a highly developed bend in the Thames.

Exit Shadwell station and turn right on Cornwall Street, then right again on Watney Street, before going right on Cable Street, passing the front entrance of the station. Stroll along the broad road for about 100m, crossing Angel Mews and passing St George's Town Hall and registry office, and then turn left into St George's Garden.

Pause here to take in the massive mural on your left, which extends right across one wall of the town hall. An extraordinary work – created by artist David Binnington Savage (and others) and stylistically inspired by the social realism of Mexican painter Diego Rivera – the mural depicts the Battle of Cable Street, which took place on 4 October 1936. This large street fight (one of several violent confrontations that took place on the same sunny Sunday) happened when the people of east London (Independent Labour Party members, Trade Unionists, British Jews and Irish labourers large among them) physically stopped the British Union of Fascists, led by Sir Oswald Mosley and protected by the police, from marching through predominantly Jewish parts of the city. This area remains richly multicultural, and although the commemorative mural has been defaced by racist and right-wing vandals several times, it's always been proudly restored.

Continue straight through the little green park, passing the impressive 300-

year-old Nicholas Hawksmoor-designed St George-in-the-East Church, with its peculiar 'pepperpot' towers, which miraculously survived a direct hit by a bomb during the Blitz. Approaching the park gate, the dilapidated building on your left is a Victorian mortuary with a connection to the infamous Whitechapel murders, a spate of unsolved crimes committed by the serial killer known as 'Jack the Ripper'; the post-mortem of Elizabeth Stride, believed to have been the Ripper's third victim, took place here after she was found murdered nearby.

Exit the park, cross the main road at the lights and walk straight along Wapping Lane. The pavement here traces the eastern edge of Tobacco Dock (on your right, behind a brick wall) where, in the 19th century, huge amounts of imported tobacco, wine and brandy were unloaded from boats and stored in vast vaults rumoured to rival the crypts of Gothic cathedrals in size.

At the wall's end, you'll be confronted by the incongruous sight of two large pirate boats. These vessels are actually replicas of real ships: the *Three Sisters* (a 330-ton merchant ship used to transport

goods from India and the West Indies, which sank in 1799) and the *Sea Lark* (an American 10-gun schooner captured by the Royal Navy, which saw action in the War of 1812 between Britain and the United States). They are remnants of a failed attempt to turn Tobacco Dock into a commercial amusement and shopping area in the 1980s. These days the revamped dock boasts a few bars, cafés and artsy outlets, and often hosts large dance events and other shindigs.

Turn right and go down the steps towards the ships and the path beside

the Ornamental Canal, from where you can enjoy a great view of the Shard.

Go left along the waterway, passing beneath Wapping Lane and following a fingerpost pointing towards Shadwell Basin. Just after a series of shallow water steps on your right you will reach Wapping Woods, a little leafy oasis amid the East End's old industrial landscape. Go straight ahead, through the trees, still following arrows for Shadwell Basin. Leave the woods and stroll along a small section of canal, passing underneath a bascule bridge and walking beside another flight of water steps.

Soon you'll meet Shadwell Basin, a large body of water adjacent to the Thames, which once formed part of the busy London Docks that dominated Wapping during the 19th century. The ever-swelling size of merchant vessels made the docks unusable by the mid-20th century, and they were closed to shipping in 1969. After a period of dereliction Shadwell Basin was completely reimagined in the 1980s, and the protected pool is now surrounded by swanky apartments and used for watersports such as canoeing, kayaking and sailing. Turn left and walk around the basin, keeping the water on your right.

Exit Shadwell Basin by a red bascule bridge, cross the road and do a dogleg, turning left by the entrance to Shadwell Basin Outdoor Activity Centre and then immediately hooking right along an alleyway, following a fingerpost for King Edward Memorial Park. Emerge on the banks of the Thames by a cluster of benches overlooking the river and the sky-tickling towers of Canary Wharf on the Isle of Dogs (straight ahead).

Turn left and wander along the Thames Path to King Edward Memorial Park, a serene and green little refuge, offering shade beneath crab apple, sweet chestnut, wild service and cigar trees, with excellent views across the river. Pass Shadwell Dock Stairs and go to the left of a pretty little circular building, which is actually just a ventilation shaft for the Rotherhithe Tunnel that runs deep under the river here. Look out for the plaque dedicated to Sir Hugh Willoughby, who set off from here in 1553 on his ill-fated expedition to try and navigate the Northeast Passage linking the Atlantic and Pacific Oceans via the top of the globe.

Walk through the centre of the gardens to the Edward VII Memorial, and then bear right. Turn left to exit the park and

go right past Free Trade Wharf by a blue plaque informing you that Captain James Cook once lived in a (long gone) house on this spot. Pass the sign for the Thames Path and Riverside Walk and go right at Atlantic Wharf, walking down Jardine Road to the riverbank, before turning left along the Thames Path. After crossing a little wooden bridge over some stone steps, you have to leave the waterside briefly to go around Keepier Wharf, just before Ratcliff Beach, but continue along Narrow Street, past the back of Sun Wharf, and then hook a right along an alley to rejoin the riverside trail. Go past Bread Street Kitchen (a Gordon Ramsay gaff) and climb the steps, before turning right to cross the bridge over the aquatic entrance to Limehouse Basin. Look left to see the lock.

If it's open, turn right through West Cobb Gate straight after the bridge to explore the Old Limehouse Cut entrance, or simply continue along Narrow Street (the path soon rejoins the road anyway). After passing Papermill Wharf and Blyth's Wharf, check out The Grapes, a wonderful old watering hole that's been quenching thirsts since 1583 (although the current building dates to the 1720s). The pub boasts a beer balcony that literally overhangs the river, from where – if you look left towards the Canary Wharf high rises – you can see Antony Gormley's *Another Time XVI* statue braving the waves in the rising and falling water of the tidal Thames.

Carry on along Narrow Street, passing Jane Ackroyd's *Herring Gull* sculpture lurking beneath a cigar tree on your left. Cut right to reach the river again via the gates into Duke Shore Wharf for a better view of Gormley's sometimes semi-submerged statue, or carry on along the road before turning right at Dunbar Wharf. Follow the Thames Path left over a curvy bridge across the entrance to Limekiln Dock.

Keep going past Dundee Wharf and when you reach Canary Wharf Pier, turn left up the steps and walk through Westferry Circus (a round garden) and

go along West India Avenue to Cabot Square. Cross the avenue at lights to walk through the centre of the square, past a fountain and numerous modern art installations, and continue into the shopping centre – a veritable cathedral of consumerism – where you will find Canary Wharf tube and DLR station.

If you have the time and energy, however, it's well worth exploring the restaurants, bars, boutiques and waterside attractions around Canary Wharf, Canada Square and Jubilee Park before you leave.

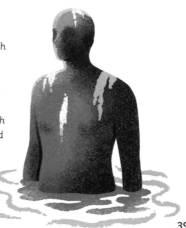

6

The Regent's Canal from Paddington to Camden

Distance 5km **Time** 2 hours
Start Paddington ⊖ ⇌
Finish Camden Town ⊖

The Regent's Canal ripples across north and east London, from Maida Vale to Limehouse Basin, where it meets the mighty Thames. Built between 1812 and 1820 to link the Grand Union Canal to the docks in east London, it was once busy with cargo-carrying barges, but is now lined with whole shoals of narrowboats and barges, and is enjoyed by paddlers, anglers and amblers.

Starting at the Paddington Basin, this route joins the wonderful waterway at its source and traces it from lovely Little Venice, past Regent's Park to the lock at Camden Town, a marvellous melting pot of market stalls serving aromatic international street food, tattoo parlours, pubs and bars, and bohemian boutiques offering everything from unique clothing and vintage vinyl to brilliantly bizarre bric-a-brac and rare books.

Leaving Paddington station, follow directions for 'Taxis' and 'Exit 3: Grand Union Canal'. (If you're coming out of the tube, head directly for Exit 3.) Walk past the taxi rank and keep going straight until you emerge on the banks of the canal. Paddington Basin, one London terminus of the Grand Union Canal, is off to your right, but this walk turns left along the towpath.

Walk with the water on your right, along a bank lined by boats, many of which are floating restaurants. Go under Bishop's Bridge and pass a blue statue of Paddington Bear and a memorial to enigmatic code-breaking genius and victim of the state, Alan Turing (who lived nearby). Keep going along the towpath, past a footbridge and under the cacophonous Westway (A40), just prior to which you'll see the uncanny couple that comprise *Standing Man* and *Walking Man*, hyper-realistic bronze figures created by sculptor Sean Henry.

Pass hordes of houseboats, over the bright bows of which you'll see the trees of little Stone Wharf park and gardens.

Go under low Harrow Road Bridge and walk along the towpath into Little Venice, from where the Grand Union Canal continues upcountry to the Midlands, while the Regent's Canal begins its journey towards the Thames.

This alluring aquatic roundabout – once called Paddington Broadwater but known as Little Venice since the name was coined by crime-writer Margery Allingham in the 1930s – has long attracted artists and performers, including Björk. Narrowboats cling to the banks and Browning's

Island, named after Victorian poet and local lad Robert Browning, is off to your right. Splayed across the far bank is Rembrandt Gardens, where painters' studios once proliferated.

At the Waterside Café (housed on a boat), go right, across the pretty blue bridge. To your left the Grand Union

The Regent's Canal from Paddington to Camden

touring and performing along London's waterways). Duck below another blue bridge, pass beneath Warwick Avenue and start strolling along the first section of the Regent's Canal.

Before long you have to leave the towpath briefly to walk along Blomfield Road with a gated marina full of narrowboats on your right, just the other side of the fence. Cross Maida Vale/ Edgware Road at the traffic lights and continue along Aberdeen Place. Astonishingly, the canal runs underground here, through the 249m-long Maida Hill Tunnel hidden beneath the buildings on your right. On a house on the left side of the road, look out for a blue plaque marking the former home of Wing Commander Guy Gibson VC, who led the RAF's 617 Squadron, 'the Dam Busters', in their audacious bouncing-bomb raid on the Ruhr Valley in 1943.

Canal leads all the way to Leicester and Birmingham, but this route turns right after stepping off the bridge. Walk along the towpath, with the water and Browning Island now on your right, past a pick-up point for the boat service to Camden, and the Puppet Theatre Barge (typically moored here, unless it's out

Just past Victoria Passage, as the road begins bending left, turn right along a small alleyway between flats and an electrical substation, crossing a Jubilee Greenway tile in the floor. As you pass an information board about the canal, the waterway comes back into sight, down

43

on your right. The path spits you out on Lisson Grove. Cross the road, turn right, then after about 50m turn left through a metal gate to rejoin the canal towpath. Walk with the water now on your left and flats on your right until a footbridge takes you across to the opposite bank.

Continue along the towpath, with the canal once again on your right, passing beneath railway lines and Park Road. The route reveals two very different sides of London in the space of a few hundred metres here, as council flats abruptly give way to massive opulent mansions that overlook Regent's Park on the right bank of the waterway. Quite suddenly you're out of the concrete jungle and walking beneath real trees, amid manicured gardens. A footpath runs parallel to the towpath, and this pretty stretch is always busy with runners, riders and walkers, while kayakers are commonly out, paddling the placid canal below the weeping willows that dangle their limbs languidly in the still water.

Enjoy this green section of towpath, ambling under the beautiful brick arches of Chalbert Bridge and Macclesfield Bridge, and walking below an aerial walkway that passes overhead, amidst the tree canopy. If your ears start picking up some incongruous roars, howls and yowls around now, don't panic, it's just the inhabitants of London Zoo making themselves known. The world's oldest scientific zoo spans the canal here, with Monkey Valley on your left and the rest of the animals housed on the Regent's Park bank, over on the right.

Keep going, walking beneath a couple of attractive metal bridges, and follow the canal around a distinct left bend in the waterway, where the iconic *Feng Shang Princess*, a large floating Chinese restaurant, is moored just across the water.

As you round the corner, the steeple of St Mark's Church points up at Primrose Hill on your left. Stroll under Regent's Park Road canal bridge, past a cluster of narrowboats. Buildings begin to line the banks again now, and as you go under Gloucester Avenue and a couple of railway bridges the surroundings start to become much more urban. The Pirate Castle activity centre, which offers kayaking and canoeing experiences to inner-city and disadvantaged kids, is on the right bank, surrounded by boats.

Just after walking beneath the Oval Road Bridge (which boasts a Banksy mural) and over the hump of a walkway, you will see the famous iron footbridge that looks out over Camden Lock. Pass the entrance to West Yard on your left (a great place to explore and grab some street food), and then stroll straight over the bridge, past the lock gates and into the colourful chaos of Camden Town.

Synonymous with counterculture, fashion and music, Camden's countless live venues and drinking dens have spawned and inspired many artists, including Madness (local lads whose nutty journey to the top began with a residency at the Dublin Castle) and Amy Winehouse, who is commemorated with a statue in the Stables Market.

Turn right to walk towards Camden Town tube station, or go any which way and get happily lost in the anarchic mess of markets, cafés, pubs, boutiques and bars.

7

The Regent's Canal from Angel to Limehouse

Distance 10km **Time** 3 hours
Start Angel ⊖
Finish Limehouse ⇌ ⊖

This walk joins the Regent's Canal at The Angel, Islington, and traces it to the terminus at Limehouse Basin, by the Thames. On the way, it explores Broadway Market and London Fields, passes the impressive pagoda in Victoria Park and crosses Mile End Park's glorious Green Bridge.

The Angel takes its name from a legendary coaching inn that stood on a busy junction in Islington for more than 300 years, after opening in 1614.

Exit from Angel tube station, turn left on Islington High Street, and left again along City Road. Cross Torrens Street and go left along Duncan Terrace, which features terraced Georgian houses on one side and modern flats on the other, with a garden corridor running through the centre. Open to all, these well-tended community gardens are full of squirrels, insect hotels, benches and interesting trees, including hazel, willow-leaved cotoneaster and a Chinese tree of heaven, home to one half of *Spontaneous City in the Tree of Heaven*, a sculptural installation formed from a cluster of ornate birdboxes (the other half occupies another tree of heaven on the opposite side of London).

Exit the first section of gardens and turn right to meet the Regent's Canal as it emerges from the darkness of the 878m-long Islington Tunnel. Walk east along the towpath, part of the Jubilee Greenway, a 60km-long waymarked walking and cycling route across London. Pass under Danbury Street Bridge and continue to the café at City Road Lock, where the waterway splits, with City Road Basin forking right. Keep left to stay on the Regent's Canal and walk under Wharf Road Bridge. Continue beneath Packington Bridge, strolling past umpteen narrowboats and a fingerpost for Shepherdess Walk Park, to reach Sturt's Lock at Union Wharf.

Go under New North Road Bridge and trace the towpath as it parallels

47

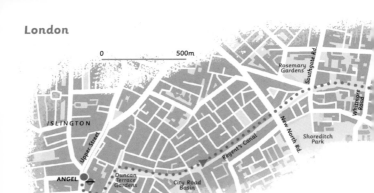

Baring Street to Southgate Road Bridge, accompanied by cawing carrion crows and croaking coots that dive under the water as you approach. Runners, dog walkers, pedallers, pram-pushers and hand-holding lovers all populate this stretch.

Pass a fingerpost for Victoria Park and Limehouse Basin. Wander under Whitmore Road Bridge, stroll along Kingsland Towpath and continue over a bridge straight ahead, with the water of Kingsland Basin (home to Hackney's houseboat community) on your left. Stoop under low Kingsland Bridge and pass beneath the railway. On the opposite bank you'll see the canoes and kayaks of Laburnum Boat Club, a community-based project providing the

people of Hackney with the opportunity to try paddling. After passing the funky modern architecture of the Bridge Academy and going under Haggerston Road Bridge, scan Hoxton Docks for *Sharks!* – an award-winning-but-polarising art installation by architect Jaimie Shorten.

Continue along the towpath as it passes under Queensbridge Road Bridge and runs alongside Regent's Row. Go past Acton's Lock to wide car-free Cat and Mutton Bridge, where you can divert to browse Broadway Market and explore London Fields. There are cafés, boutique bakeries, bars and eateries all along Broadway Market, including the Cat and Mutton pub at the top of the Broadway, which has been serving pints since 1729. You'll find public toilets in

London Fields, an area of common ground with a lido and lots of open-access sports facilities. If you venture this far, check out the *Flower Sellers* sculpture on the right as you enter the park.

Rejoin the towpath and continue east. Go under a high railway bridge and low Cambridge Heath Bridge, pass a fingerpost for Victoria Park and Limehouse Basin, and follow Pound Path until you reach Canal Gate, leading into Victoria Park. Also known as the 'People's Park', this is London's oldest public park. It opened in 1845 to provide access to green space for the East End's working class, and is accessible 7am to dusk daily (if it's shut, you can simply continue along the canal towpath).

Enter via the Canal Gate and bear right, following a fingerpost pointing towards the lakeside Pavilion Café, Chinese Pagoda and East Park. Cross the sealed track, with Bonner Gate and

bridge to your right, passing the statues of *The Dogs of Alcibiades* on your left. After another 100m, bear left and cross the bridge to Pagoda Island, where a charming tiered structure overlooks the tranquil ornamental lake. Built for a Chinese exhibition at Hyde Park Corner in 1842, the original pagoda was relocated to Victoria Park in 1847, but after being damaged during WWII it was demolished in the 1950s. The present pagoda was unveiled in 2011.

Leave Pagoda Island over a second bridge, bear right and walk with the pond on your right, looking for water birds including Mandarin ducks, red-crested pochards, little grebes, kingfishers and grey heron. Continue past the Pavilion Café, where you'll find toilets and drinking water. Crown Gate West is on your left, but continue with the lake on your right, passing *Skyscraper* and *Bird*, an intriguing pair of sculptures

49

that emerge from the water, by Romanian artist Ernö Bartha. Bear left to exit the park via Cricketers' Gate. Carefully cross Old Ford Road, turn right, then immediate left up Stoneway Walk to rejoin the Regent's Canal towpath.

Follow the fingerpost for Limehouse Basin and go under Roman Road Bridge, passing the *Fishtail* and *Bow Bottle* sculptures on your left. Also to the left, reeds and rushes grow around pretty ponds, amid the greenery that marks the start of Mile End Park. Pass the Palm Tree pub and more artwork, including the *Portrait Bench*, and walk under a pedestrian bridge.

After going under a railway bridge, it's worth straying left to explore the linear green space that is Mile End Park. Climb straight over the prominent Art Mound and cross the Green Bridge – an innovative cycle- and walkway, complete with grass and trees – which spans busy Mile End Road, before rejoining the canal at Gunmaker's Arms Bridge. (If you'd rather stick to the towpath, just carry on

past Mile End Lock, go under Mile End Road Bridge and continue beneath Gunmaker's Arms Bridge.)

Meander past Johnson's Lock – where wildflowers thrive in community gardens, herons hunt and swans preen by modern sculptures – and continue under Grey Crescent Bridge. Pass a fingerpost for the nearby Ragged School Museum (housed in the old premises of Dr Barnardo's Copperfield Road Ragged School, which opened in 1877 to offer Mile End children a basic education), and continue along the canal towards Limehouse Basin.

Walk past a tall brick chimney, go under the railway bridge and continue to Salmon Lane Lock. Go under a footbridge, Salmon Lane Bridge and Commercial Road Bridge to reach Commercial Road Lock. You can turn right and walk over the footbridge directly to Limehouse station, but it's well worth exploring Limehouse Basin, an historic industrial dock that's evolved into a modern marina where narrowboats bob alongside expensive yachts.

Loop the basin, keeping the water on your right. Spot the apparently levitating figure of 'Christ the Steersman' atop Our Lady Immaculate and Saint Frederick Church, which was deliberately designed to be visible from the basin and to resemble a ship figurehead to reinforce the maritime theme. Wander over the footbridge, where an information sign describes the dock's wildlife. To your left, Limehouse Cut leads to Ropemakers Field and beyond that Canada Wharf can be seen across the Thames.

Carry on to Limehouse Basin Lock, which connects the tidal Thames to over 1000 miles of navigable waterways. To sneak a peak at the broad majestic river, go over the road and through West Cobb Gate. When you're ready, cross the footbridge over Limehouse Basin Lock and walk with the water on your right until you reach Limehouse DLR station.

8

Primrose Hill and Regent's Park

Distance 4.5km **Time** 2 hours
Start Chalk Farm ⊖
Finish Baker Street ⊖

Walk from the vibrant venues, colourful crescents and chic cafés of Chalk Farm and Primrose Hill – home to political theorists, poets and Paddington Bear – past a picturesque viewpoint overlooking London, before descending across Henry VIII's old hunting chase and passing through one of the capital's great parks to arrive at the doorstep of Britain's favourite fictional sleuth.

Leave Chalk Farm tube station and emerge on Adelaide Road. The Roundhouse, a former railway engine shed transformed into a lively music venue, is just 100m away (down Haverstock Hill/Chalk Farm Road towards Camden), but this route turns right on Adelaide Road. Use the zebra crossing and then turn left along Bridge Approach. Stroll over the wide bridge spanning the railway lines to arrive

by Pembroke Castle pub at the point where King Henry's Road segues into Gloucester Avenue.

You're now in the affluent and artsy neighbourhood of Primrose Hill, where the attractive Victorian-era terraces have housed many notable names over the years. There are blue plaques aplenty beside doorways along these tidy streets. The main route continues straight ahead to walk along Regent's Park Road, passing the one-time abode of the political philosopher Friedrich Engels at No 122 and strolling past all sorts of beautiful boutiques, bistros and bookshops, before meeting Primrose Hill Road.

However, lovers of literature and verse interested in visiting an address that tragically ties together the Irish poet and dramatist W B Yeats and the American writer Sylvia Plath might want to take the following short diversion. From the Pembroke Castle, go left along Gloucester Avenue and turn right on Fitzroy Road. Pass the Princess of Wales pub, cross Chalcot

London

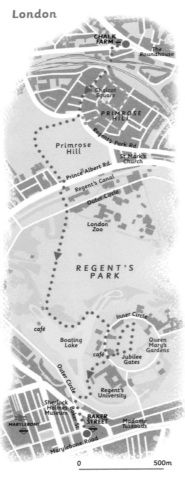

Road and continue very briefly along Fitzroy Road to number 23, just past the junction on your left. A young Yeats lived in this house and the blue plaque commemorating this (put up in 1957) attracted Sylvia Plath to rent accommodation at the same address in late 1962, and it was here she took her own life the following year, aged just 30. This awful event isn't marked, but return to Chalcot Road, turn left and walk to Chalcot Square. Opposite this tiny green park, at No 3, you will find a plaque to Plath, who shared this house with her husband (later poet laureate) Ted Hughes during an earlier period, when she produced her first volume of poetry, *The Colossus*, and wrote her semi-autobiographical novel, *The Bell Jar*. From here, go left and trace the arc of Chalcot Crescent – a pretty and colourful street that you might recognise as the residence of the Browns in the *Paddington* films – before emerging on Regent's Park Road. Turn right and walk up to the junction with Primrose Hill Road, where you rejoin the main route.

Cross Regent's Park Road and briefly walk up Primrose Hill Road. After a few metres, turn left through the gate into the delightful grassy park that rises to the top of Primrose Hill proper. This elevated expanse of open land, punctuated by small pockets of trees, was originally a chase used by Henry VIII for hunting. Subsequently it was owned by Eton College, until it was bought by the Crown Estate and turned into an area for outdoor recreation for the people of north London by an Act of Parliament. Once upon a time duels were fought here, with pistols drawn at dawn, prize-fighting bouts took place and public hangings happened in front of large crowds, but now you'll find an altogether more serene scene, populated by picnickers, canoodlers and kite flyers.

Take the sealed path leading right (not the dirt path hard right that runs parallel to the road) and ascend to the 63m-high head of the hill, where a stone is inscribed with some apposite words from the ever-eloquent Londoner William Blake: 'I have conversed with the spiritual sun. I saw him on Primrose Hill'.

This popular spot offers stunning panoramic views across the capital and out past Hampstead on a good day.

Looking towards central London, the distinct stiletto steeple of St Mark's Church is slightly to your left, rising above a small cluster of trees standing in the park, which include in their ranks an oak known as Shakespeare's Tree, originally planted in 1864, reportedly in front of a 100,000-strong crowd, to mark the 300th anniversary of the Bard's birth (but replaced in 1964, after the first died).

Continue along the path, curving left and strolling down the hill, ignoring several turnings to the right. Opposite a park entrance by the corner of Ormonde and St Edmund's Terraces, three paths lead left – disregard these and keep going straight until you reach a park gate by a little house. There's an outdoor gym, playground and public toilet block over to your left, but this route exits the park here and crosses Prince Albert Road via the zebra crossing. Do a dogleg (right, then left), following signs for London Zoo.

Walk over Regent's Canal via pretty Primrose Hill Bridge (an iron pedestrian bridge), cross the Outer Circle (a road) and enter Regent's Park. Like Primrose

Hill, this was once part of the immense Forest of Middlesex, before Henry VIII made it his happy hunting ground, part of a semi-wild expanse known as Marylebone Park. Eventually, after being sculpted into the more planned park you see today by the architect John Nash in the early 1800s, the renamed Regent's Park was opened to the public in the mid-19th century. It's now home to a large zoo, acres of grassland and meadow, around 5000 varieties of tree, more than 120 bird species, London's largest outdoor sports area, fantastically florid rose gardens and the Big Smoke's only breeding population of hedgehogs.

After the Outer Circle the path splits three ways; take the track leading right and stroll through the park towards the boating lake. You cross a couple of other paths, but keep going straight, walking with a woodland on your right after the second crosspaths, until you pass a pubic toilet block and meet the water, where an information board details the birds that inhabit the lake. You can cross a brace of blue bridges here, hopping over Hanover Island to peruse the Waterside Café and perhaps hire a rowing boat or pedalo (April–October), but this walk bears left.

Walk with the water and a tree-covered island on your right, looking out for wildlife and waterfowl, and then turn right across Longbridge. On the far side, go straight ahead and cross the Inner Circle (another road). Turn right and walk along the pavement for about 100m, passing the entry gate for the Regent's Park Open Air Theatre, until you reach an entrance to Queen Mary's Gardens on your left. Enter, passing the Regent's Bar and Kitchen, and follow a sign pointing left for the Open Air Theatre. Pass the alfresco amphitheatre (on your left) to reach the impressive William McMillan-designed Triton and Dryads Fountain. Circle this flowing feature and then stroll down the broad bench-lined main track towards the ornately gilded Jubilee Gates. To your left lie the epic flower gardens, where some 12,000 roses aromatically bloom in season. Closer to the gate, also on the left, floats the Japanese Garden Island.

When you've finished exploring, leave

the gardens by following fingerposts pointing towards Baker Street and the Boating Lake. Go back past the Regent's Bar and Kitchen, cross over the Inner Circle road and walk straight ahead, through a gate, following signs for Baker Street tube. Pass a bandstand on the way to the lake, bear left along the bank and then turn right to cross Clarence Bridge. On the far side, go right and then left, still following fingerposts pointing towards Baker Street tube.

The end of the walk is elementary: continue straight along Baker Street, passing the Sherlock Holmes museum on your right to reach the tube station, which is fronted by a large bronze statue of the pipe-puffing sleuth.

Arthur Conan Doyle's Sherlock Holmes resided at 221B Baker Street, and in 1990 the museum dedicated to this enduringly popular character was officially assigned this address (which previously belonged to a branch of the Abbey National Bank, who had to employ someone in the role of 'secretary to Sherlock Holmes' to respond to the bundles of mail they received addressed to the fictional drug-taking detective). A blue plaque adorns the wall of the museum, commemorating Holmes as if he were a real person.

9

Hyde Park to Trafalgar Square

Distance 5–6km **Time** 2–3 hours
Start Lancaster Gate ⊖
Finish St James's Park ⊖
or Charing Cross ⊖ ⇌

Despite its Big Smoke moniker, London is one of the world's most verdant major metropolises, with thousands of grassy parks punctuating the tarmac, concrete and glass of the urban street-scape. This walk explores the capital's green heart, tracing a chain of interlinked central parks from the edge of Kensington Gardens, across Hyde Park, over Constitution Hill, around Green Park, past Buckingham Palace and through St James's Park to arrive at Trafalgar Square.

Leave Lancaster Gate tube and turn right, walking across Lancaster Terrace. Use the traffic lights to cross Bayswater Road to Marlborough Gate, which leads into a great green expanse right on the invisible seam between Kensington Gardens and Hyde Park.

Bear slightly left to enter Hyde Park proper. Pass a café and walk with the fantastic fountains and four resplendent rectangular pools of the Italian Garden on your right. Continue past a statue of vaccine pioneer Edward Jenner and follow the path along the bank of The Long Water, with the lake on your right. Look out for parakeets, colourful visitors that thrive in London parks, and native grey heron, which stalk the waterside. The trees lining the lake are home to many animals, from Cetti's warbler, tiny wood mice and little owls to beautiful butterflies, including peacock, tortoiseshell and painted lady.

Just past a little shelter you'll reach *The Arch*, a large stone sculpture by Henry Moore that occupies a gap in the trees by the lake, framing another artwork (*Physical Energy*, a bronze equestrian statue by Victorian artist George Frederic Watts) over on the Kensington Gardens bank. When the path forks, bear left and ascend to meet Serpentine Bridge. Carefully cross the road, turn right along the bridge and look left to take in the curvaceous length of the Serpentine. Created at the behest of Queen Caroline, wife of King George II, this 40-acre lake dates to 1730 and is loved by waterbirds and outdoor swimmers alike (it was used for aquatic events during the 2012 London Olympics).

Reaching the end of the bridge, turn left and descend to the side of the Serpentine by *Isis*, a large depiction of an Egyptian goddess in bird form. Keep walking with the water on your left and the Diana Princess of Wales Memorial Fountain on the right, full of squealing children on hot days. Pass another café and bar, and the Serpentine Lido, open to all in summer (entry fee) but used by hardy club swimmers year round (including during the annual Peter Pan Cup Christmas Day Race).

At the eastern end of the lake, past an urn-shaped memorial to Queen Caroline, is the large Serpentine Bar & Kitchen. If you continued straight on across Serpentine Road and into the northern part of Hyde Park,

you'd reach the Reformer's Tree monument and Speakers' Corner, both highly symbolic features on the landscape of British politics. However, this route takes an acute right turn at the café and then an immediate left to wander through The Dell, just to the left of the poignant Holocaust Memorial. Continue to and through Hyde Park Rose Garden, passing Lady Feodora Gleichen's fountain statue of *Diana the Huntress* and a pergola that booms with blooms in summertime, and exit just beyond Alexander Munro's *Boy and Dolphin* fountain. Go straight ahead, cross South Carriage Drive at the lights (beware of bikes) and follow arrows for Green Park.

Enter Hyde Park Corner (surely

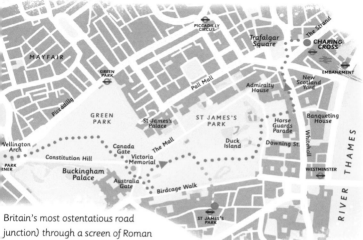

Britain's most ostentatious road junction) through a screen of Roman revival-style arches. Continue straight ahead at the lights, then bear left to cross Grosvenor Place and walk towards Wellington Arch, designed by Decimus Burton and topped by Adrian Jones' *Peace Descending on the Quadriga of War*, a bronze sculpture depicting Nike, the Ancient Greek Goddess of Victory, riding a four-horse chariot, which replaced a statue of the Duke of Wellington after the whole arch was moved a short distance from its original spot in 1882–83. Pass the Royal Artillery Memorial on the right and a different statue of the de-perched duke on your

left, before ambling through the great green gates of the arch.

Walk past the stone Commonwealth Memorial Gates, where bicycles and bipeds are mercifully directed onto different tracks, into Green Park. By a park map, bear left (but not acute left) and walk through Queen's Meadow, seasonally festooned by blooming wildflowers. At the next crosspaths, turn right and wander beneath the branches of towering London plane trees to a confluence of paths beneath a tall lamp where an information board details the park's avian occupants. Turn right at the lamppost and walk down towards Buckingham Palace. Pass the maple leaf-layered memorial to Canadian servicemen killed during WWI and WWII on your left, and exit Green Park at Canada Gate.

Cross Constitution Hill at the lights and walk in front of the royal residence of Buckingham Palace with the Victoria Memorial on your left, crowned by a gilded bronze effigy of Victoria, the Roman goddess of Victory, and surrounded by marine-themed statues symbolising Britain's naval strength. Cross the road to reach the kangaroo-adorned Australia Gate and turn right to cross Spur Road at the lights. Turn right again to meet Birdcage Walk with the entrance to St James's Park on the corner. Bear left and walk around the lake with the water on your right.

In the early 17th century, St James's Park (named after a medieval hospital dedicated to St James the Less) contained a menagerie of incongruous animals, including an elephant, crocodiles and camels, and an aviary of exotic birds, kept for the amusement of the monarch, King James I (James VI of Scotland). The park was redesigned by John Nash in the early 19th century and those big beasts are long gone, but conspicuous among the lake's many waterfowl is a posse of pelicans, resident here since 1664 when a Russian ambassador gifted them to Charles II. Turn right to cross the park's Blue Bridge, enjoying views left across the tree-covered banks and Duck Island (a beautiful sight in the blush of autumn) to Horse Guards Parade, with the London Eye in the background.

Leaving the bridge you have two options: to bail early, walk straight, exit the park just past a water fountain, cross Birdcage Walk (a road named after the aforementioned aviary), then go directly along Queen Anne's Gate and over Broadway–Petty France at the zebra crossing to St James's Park tube station. Alternatively, turn left and follow a fingerpost pointing towards the Churchill War Rooms, walking with the water on your left, past a fountain, to the lake's eastern end. The War Rooms are straight ahead, but this route traces the curve of the bank left, passing lovely little Duck

Island Cottage with its vegetable garden. The island once hosted a bomb-disposal unit, but it's green and serene now.

When the path forks, leave the lake and go straight ahead. Turn right at the Guards Memorial, cross Horse Guards Road and march across Horse Guards Parade, a jousting arena in Henry VIII's time and now the site of numerous ceremonial shenanigans. The giant gravel quadrangle is flanked by military monuments and government buildings collectively known as Whitehall, including Admiralty Citadel, an odd-looking ivy-clad bomb-proof bunker to your left, which leads to a labyrinth of secret subterranean tunnels used during wartime.

Walk straight ahead through the arches of the Household Cavalry Museum building to emerge opposite

Banqueting House, the only surviving part of the Palace of Whitehall, main residence of English monarchs for much of the 16th and 17th centuries, which burned down in 1698. King Charles I was beheaded in the street here on the afternoon of 30 January 1649.

Downing Street, the modern seat of power, is just up the road to the right, but this route goes left, past Admiralty House (on the left) and Scotland Yard (right), historic headquarters of the Metropolitan Police, towards Trafalgar Square. Pass the Equestrian Statue of Charles I, from where distances to and from London from everywhere else in the country are calculated, and continue to Nelson's Column. The National Gallery is directly ahead and Charing Cross tube station is off to the right, along the Strand.

10

Holland Park to Notting Hill

Distance 6km **Time** 2–3 hours
Start Holland Park ⊖
Finish Ladbroke Grove ⊖

**From the gardens of Holland Park
– an historic and harmonious
haven hidden in the heart of
central London – along the
pavements, through the parkland
and past the palace of Kensington
to the art-imbued streets of
Notting Hill and treasure-laced
marketplace of Portobello Road,
this west London wander is as
vibrant, varied and vivacious as
a carnival float in August. It's a
three-act rambling route you can
do all at once or in separate
sections, with multiple hop-off
points along the way.**

The walk starts in the posh part of
Notting Hill. Leave Holland Park tube
station and cross the road at the traffic
lights. Turn left along broad Holland Park
Avenue and walk up to the first turning
on the right, Holland Park, where
St Volodymyr (ruler of Ukraine 980–

1015) stands guard on the far corner,
outside the Ukrainian Institute. Turn
right along the road, lined with grand,
gleaming-white stucco-fronted Victorian
villas valued at eye-watering amounts.
(Richard Branson, Elton John, Robbie
Williams and the Beckhams have all
called Holland Park home.)

Trace the arc of the road to an elegant
curving white wall, with a series of
windows and a small door below the old
London County Council's coat of arms.
This is the northern 'Sun trap' entrance
to Holland Park, and going through the
door transports you into an immense
walled gardenscape that feels utterly
apart from the city streets outside. Now
a 22-hectare green space open to the
public, Holland Park occupies the old
grounds of a Jacobean mansion called
Cope Castle, built around 1605 for
Sir Walter Cope, Chancellor of the
Exchequer under King James I. The
building became Holland House when
the entire estate passed to Henry Rich,
1st Earl of Holland, on his marriage to
Cope's daughter Isabel.

Pass Jonathan Loxley's oval-shaped *Tonda* sculpture, bear slightly right and walk up a slope. At the fingerpost, take the track leading virtually straight ahead (bending slightly right), following the arm pointing towards Opera Holland Park, Holland House and Garden, and Dutch Garden. Amble along the tree-fringed footpath until you meet a seated statue of Henry Vassall-Fox, 3rd Baron Holland, a prominent 19th-century Whig politician and conflicted abolitionist who ended up inheriting (through his wife) several slave estates in Jamaica, for which he received compensation when the barbaric trade eventually ended.

Turn right, following the fingerpost for the Kyoto Garden. Walk gently downhill and turn left at the next junction, then left again to enter the exquisitely designed area sculpted to resemble a traditional Japanese garden, with waterfalls, a peaceful pond populated by koi carp, stone lanterns and delicate Japanese maple trees. Do a clockwise loop of these lovely gardens – a gift from the city of Kyoto (Japan's cultural capital) in 1991 – crossing the bridge and passing a water feature fringed with colourful Japanese flora. Hungry heron are often here, eyeing the fish, while peacocks imperiously prowl around the place. At the far end of the pond, before you reach the bamboo fence, bear left and exit through the Fukushima Garden, another gift from Japan, this time in thanks for support after the earthquake, tsunami and nuclear nightmare that struck Fukushima in 2011.

Turn left again and walk with a wall on your right. Ignore steps leading right and continue towards Holland House, which was badly damaged by bombs during the Blitz in WWII. Just before the remains of the mansion (part of which now houses a youth hostel), turn right and follow a pointer for 'Opera Holland Park, café and Dutch Gardens'. Go through a wisteria arch, turn right and explore the sculptures, flowers and fountains of these meticulously maintained gardens. Just before a giant chessboard, head left down steps to a fountain, and then go left again. Leave the gardens by turning right through a brick arch into the forecourt of the Holland Park Café. Call in for a cuppa or continue by going left and walking in front of the space where open-air operatic performances are staged during summer. At a fingerpost turn right, following the arrow for the Design Museum and walking down a

broad track lined by London plane trees, with playing fields on your right.

Pass the funky-looking Design Museum and leave the park through ornamental iron gates to emerge on Kensington High Street. Turn left and pound the pavement for about 500m. If you're exhausted after exploring Holland Park, you can bail at High Street Kensington tube station on your right, but act two of this route starts by turning left just past the tube, by the Ivy Kensington Brasserie, to stroll along Kensington Church Walk,

which leaves the busy road and sends you though peaceful gardens and around St Mary Abbots Church (built in the 19th century, but with roots that extend back a further 600 years). Keep going, past several crafty boutiques, to a T-junction, then go right on Holland Street. Cross Kensington Church Street at the lights and go straight ahead along York House Place, following a fingerpost for Kensington Gardens and Palace. Continue through York Passage (which belongs to the Crown Estate, and has a gate that shuts at dusk) and emerge opposite Kensington Palace Green.

Cross the road and green, and go through the Studio Gates to enter Kensington Park. Stroll along Studio Walk with Kensington Palace on your left, behind ornate gates. Built in 1605, this Jacobean mansion became a royal residence in 1689 when William III (of Orange fame) and Mary II moved in to ease the asthma that frail William was experiencing in Whitehall Palace. Queen Victoria spent an unhappy childhood here and after being crowned quickly moved to Buckingham Palace, where

successive monarchs have based themselves ever since. Charles and Diana lived here as Prince and Princess of Wales, and Princes William and Harry both grew up in the palace, where William and his family still reside.

At a T-junction, turn left along Broad Walk and stroll past the front of the palace and the Queen Victoria statue on your left (or do a loop of the imaginatively named Round Pond on your right). Reaching a fingerpost, you could continue straight ahead to leave the park through Black Lion Gate and finish at Queensway tube, but this route follows the arm pointing left to pass the Diana Memorial playground and Elfin Oak (the stump of a 900-year-old tree carved with mythical creatures and animals). Carry on until you reach Orme Square Gate and exit the park onto Bayswater Road. Turn left and walk 500m to Notting Hill Gate tube station.

To continue on the walk's third and final act, stroll straight past the tube entrance, following signs for Portobello Market, and turn right along Pembridge Road. At the mini roundabout, keep right and use the zebra crossing just beyond it to cross to the left side of Pembridge Road. Amble along the left pavement, passing umpteen excellent coffee outlets to The Sun in Splendour pub. Turn left along Portobello Road, a colourful thoroughfare famous for its antique shops and sensational street market, which is especially vibrant on Saturdays. Look out for a blue plaque on the wall of No 22 (on your right). The unheated attic apartment of this address was where Eric Blair – better known as George Orwell, author of *Animal Farm, 1984* and a wealth of other mostly political books, essays and articles – lived when he first arrived in London. Pass Chepstow Villas and continue along the busier bit of Portobello Road, passing iconic Alice's Antiques shop (which starred as Gruber's Antiques in the *Paddington* films). The road here is lined with curio and hat shops, tattoo parlours, bookstores and bars.

Continue across Westbourne Grove for more of the same, and then, after you cross Elgin Crescent, Portobello Road Market proper starts, with vocal vendors selling everything from street food and fresh vegetables to vintage threads and rare records.

Continue over Blenheim Crescent and, by The Castle pub, head left along Westbourne Park Road. Just past the junction, on the right side of the road, you might recognise a blue front door made famous in the film *Notting Hill* (although the original has apparently been flogged off). Continue along Westbourne Park Road, then turn right on Ladbroke Grove, a legendary London street with a long association with counter-culture and music, which is one of the major thorough-fares for floats during the Notting Hill Carnival each summer. The tube station is 150m down the road, by the bridge.

11

Belgravia to Battersea

Distance 5km **Time** 2 hours
Start Sloane Square ⊖
Finish Battersea Park ⇌

From swanky Sloane Square on the opulent edge of Belgravia, this walk saunters along the fashionable length of King's Road into the chic heart of Chelsea, before crossing the Thames via shaky Albert Bridge and exploring Battersea Park, a lush Victorian-era recreation area that's become a much greener breathing space since the chimneys of the iconic power station next door gave up smoking.

Exit Sloane Square tube to reach the plaza itself, which has enjoyed/endured an association with ostentatious wealth and flashy fashion since the 1980s, epitomised by so-called 'Sloane Rangers', an upper-class clique that stereotypically drives around town in Chelsea tractors (Land Rovers and other SUVs). Turn left and stroll around the pleasant tree-dotted quadrangle, centred around a Venus fountain,

which is named after Anglo-Irish physician, traveller and collector Hans Sloane, sometimes spuriously credited as the inventor of chocolate milk (although locals in Jamaica, where the doctor 'discovered' his recipe, had long been drinking cacao-and-dairy concoctions). After returning from the Caribbean, where he'd married into a wealthy plantation-owning family, Sloane purchased lots of land around Chelsea (including the Physic Garden encountered later), using money that at least partly came from the slave trade, and his name crops up all over the street map.

Cross Lower Sloane Street, pass the Ralph Lauren shop and continue straight along King's Road, with Duke of York Square to your left and the giant Peter Jones store on the right. Dating to the reign of Charles II, and originally a private royal road, King's Road opened to the hoi polloi in 1830. During the 1960s and '70s it was connected to waves of counter-culture and fashion, with mini-skirted models, Mods, hippies and punks populating its

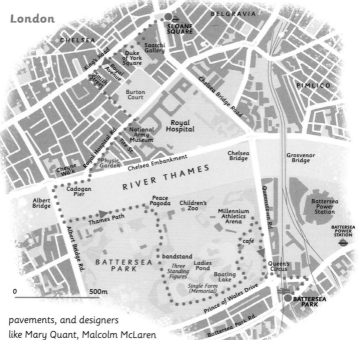

like Mary Quant, Malcolm McLaren
and Vivienne Westwood opening
daring boutiques. You can still spot
the occasional trendsetter strutting
their stuff, but there's more evidence
of rampant gentrification than sartorial
provocation these days.

Opposite Cadogan Gardens, duck
along an alley into Duke of York
Square, passing Allister Bowtell's
playful *Two Pupils* statue. Turn right in

the square and do a flyby of the
Saatchi Gallery, a treasure trove of
contemporary art since the mid-1980s,
when it pioneered the work of Damien
Hirst and the Young British Artists.
Continue through the plaza, bearing
right to rejoin King's Road.

Cross Walpole Street and pass
Royal Avenue on your left. This wide

boulevard was designed in 1682 by Christopher Wren to connect Royal Hospital Chelsea with Kensington Palace, but the project stalled at the junction with King's Road when Charles II died in 1685. Continue past Wellington Square to Smith Street; spot the blue plaque revealing where P L Travers – creator of *Mary Poppins* – lived and worked for 20 years (this is where Walt Disney pleaded with the Australian author for the rights to make the books – beloved by Disney's daughters – into a film). On the other side of King's Road, another blue plaque marks the spot where Mary Quant opened her revolutionary clothing boutique, Bazaar, in 1955.

Turn left and walk along Smith Street to St Leonard's Terrace; *Dracula* author Bram Stoker lived at No 18, off to the left, but this route crosses the road and goes straight along Durham Place, which segues into Ormonde Gate. To your left sprawls Burton Court, part of the Royal Hospital Chelsea, home of the Chelsea Pensioners. Veterans have been looked after in this old soldiers' retirement home since 1682,

a charitable concept rumoured to have been suggested by Nell Gwyn, Charles II's long-term mistress. At the end, opposite the main hospital, turn right and walk along Royal Hospital Road.

Pass the National Army Museum (with a battle tank outside) and continue across Tite Street and Paradise Walk to reach Swan Walk and the fascinating Chelsea Physic Garden. Originally established in 1673 by the Worshipful Society of Apothecaries, this unique walled botanical garden contains more than 4500 species of medicinal, herbal, edible and poisonous plants. Open to visitors every day except Saturday (there's an entrance fee), it's an interesting place and a calm space to pause and ponder.

Continue along Royal Hospital Road towards the Thames. At the junction with Cheyne Walk, a house on your right has a blue plaque noting the author George Eliot (Mary Ann Evans) died here in 1880. Carry on to the main road, cross at the lights and turn right along the riverside path. Pass Chelsea Embankment Gardens and, opposite

Cadogan Pier, ascend the steps to Albert Bridge. A sign warns marching troops to break step while crossing the bridge, lest the vibration of their synchronised footfall should cause the structure to collapse. Albert Bridge has spanned the Thames since 1873, but it's long been known as 'the Trembling Lady' because it shivers when large groups cross, and every vehicle seems to induce another wobble.

Distract yourself by looking left to contemplate Battersea Power Station (dormant since 1983), an unlovely but strangely alluring south London landmark for almost a century. Originally built with two chimneys, with a second pair added in the 1950s, the power station likely survived WWII because the Luftwaffe used the structure and the plumes of smoke it produced to navigate.

Leaving Albert Bridge, turn left into Battersea Park and ramble along the riverside with the water on your left and the wonderfully woody park extending to your right. There are over 4000 trees here, with dozens of species represented, ranging from London planes to maple, hornbeam, Persian ironwood, swamp cypress, oriental sweetgum and dawn redwood. Prior to the park being built and opened to the public in 1858, this area was known as Battersea Fields and several duels were fought here, including one in 1829 between the Duke of Wellington (British Prime Minister at the time) and the Earl of Winchilsea. Now it's a place of urban escapism, healthy recreation and quiet reflection.

At the poignant Peace Pagoda (built in 1984–85 by an order of Japanese Buddhist monks to mark the anniversary of atomic bombs being dropped on Hiroshima and Nagasaki), turn right and follow arrows for the Festival Gardens and Bandstand. Wander through a colourful area created for the 1951 Festival of Britain, Battersea Park's most prestigious moment. Pass toilets on your right, and keep walking away from the river until you reach a large circular area with a bandstand in the middle. Cross Central Avenue and go straight ahead along a meandering path to the Boating Lake. Away to your left is *Three Standing*

Figures, a Henry Moore sculpture unveiled in 1950, but this walk goes right, passing palms and exotic shrubs in the Subtropical Gardens.

Keep the water on your left, turning left at the next junction and taking in a view of the power station across the lake. Pass *Single Form (Memorial)* by Barbara Hepworth. A sibling of the artist's most famous work, which fronts the United Nations New York HQ, this sculpture was created in memory of UN Secretary-General Dag Hammarskjöld after his untimely death. Follow the lakeside to the Pear Tree Café, then bear right. At the fingerpost, go straight ahead, crossing Carriage Drive East and walking between an outdoor gym and a children's playground, towards the Millennium Athletics Arena. Upon meeting a wooden post with a Thames Path waymarker, turn right.

Follow Thames Path posts out of the park via the Rosery Gate. Go left and trace the curve of Queen's Circus roundabout, crossing Queenstown Road before turning left along Prince of Wales Drive and passing under the railway bridge through a subway illustrated with murals of microscopic pond life. At the junction with Battersea Park Road, turn left to go and explore Battersea Power Station – which has been transformed into an epic shopping plaza, eating arena and leisure centre – or catch the tube at the building's dedicated underground station (300m along the road). Alternatively, turn right for the railway stations Battersea Park (100m ahead, under the bridge) and Queenstown Road (350m further on, signed).

Putney Bridge and Barnes

Distance 10km **Time** 3 hours 30
Start & Finish Putney Bridge ⊖

From the scenic surrounds of Bishop's Park and Fulham Palace – secret sanctuaries hidden in the heart of the city – this river-jumping jaunt explores both banks of the Thames as it passes through Fulham, Hammersmith, Barnes and Putney, revealing an abundance of wildlife and riparian riches along the way. Multiple hop-off points are possible if you'd prefer to stroll it in stages.

Leave Putney Bridge tube station, turn left and then go right along Ranelagh Gardens. Bear left at Carrara Wharf as you meet Fulham High Street, then follow signage for Fulham Palace along Willow Bank as it arcs right and threads through an arch of Putney Bridge to emerge in Bishop's Park and Fulham Palace Gardens, a serene riverside spot. Pass a water fountain and the James Wedgwood statues *Adoration* and *Protection* in little gardens on the left, and continue through gates with All Saints Church on your right. Go straight ahead, past a map of the gardens and Pryor's Bank Pavilion, a mock-Tudor Victorian-era house, on your left.

To the right, a gate leads into Fulham Palace House and Garden, the Bishop of London's main residence from the 11th century until 1973. This peaceful green haven, with wonderful walled gardens and orchards, is home to some of London's most extraordinary trees, including a 450-year-old holm oak. Under Bishop Henry Compton (1675–1713), thousands of plant species were cultivated here, including the first magnolias ever grown in English soil. Open daily from dawn to dusk, it's free to wander around.

If you do go in, follow the entrance path and then go straight ahead, into the walled gardens. Walk through the middle and do a dogleg (right, then left) to leave the gardens via low Tudor Gate and cross the main lawn. Skirt the Tudor-era palace, much of which dates to the reign of Henry VII (1485–1509), keeping the building on your left. Leave via the main entrance/exit, passing the Gothic

77

Lodge and Coachman's Lodge to emerge back into Bishop's Park, before bearing left and going past a skatepark to rejoin the riverside path.

Alternatively, if the palace doesn't appeal and you'd prefer to stay by the river, continue past the gate and walk with rose gardens on your left. Just

beyond these blooms, bear left to pass a poignant memorial to locals who joined the International Brigade to fight fascism in the Spanish Civil War during the 1930s. Join the sandy path that traces the river wall and turn right, walking with the Thames on your immediate left.

Beyond the palace, and down a set of steps, another section of Bishop's Park opens up on your right, with fountains, flowerbeds and an ornamental lake.

Trace the Thames Path as it skirts a meadow and runs around the newly redeveloped Riverside Stand of Fulham Football Club's Craven Cottage stadium, scenically situated beside the water.

Continue along the bank, past Rowberry Mead, once a historic homestead and cherry orchard, now a modern riverside park with benches and a basketball court. Around the pretty Crabtree pub at Palace Wharf, spot cormorants occupying moorings on the river, wings outstretched and still like feathered Christ the Redeemer statues as they dry off, post plunge. Pass Thames Wharf Studios, where restaurants bustle and businesses hustle, and look left to

see the former Furniture Harrods Depository buildings on the far bank, now transformed into Harrods Village, a vast riverside residential development.

Keep going towards the green sheen of Hammersmith Bridge which, dating to 1887, is one of the world's oldest suspension bridges. Pass a memorial to William Tierney Clark, its engineer, who would doubtless be disappointed to hear about the bridge's recent dramas, which saw it closed in 2020 amid structural concerns, before reopening in 2021 but only for pedestrians and pedallers.

On the river, rowers regularly skim past. Since the mid-19th century, this stretch of the Thames has hosted the annual boat race between Oxford and Cambridge Universities' open-weight eights, with the rival Blues battling it out along the Championship Course to gain an advantage before passing beneath Hammersmith Bridge, where crowds assemble to cheer.

Wander past Rick Kirby's *Figurehead* sculpture and pass Fulham Reach Boat Club and a statue of Capability Brown, the 18th-century landscaping and garden guru who lived by the river in

Hammersmith. Pass the BBC's Riverside Studios — where classic programmes including *Doctor Who*, *Hancock's Half Hour* and *Blue Peter* have been made — and continue along Beckett's Wharf Riverside Walk to Hammersmith Bridge. Climb the steps here, and cross the Thames.

On the south bank, you have a choice. For the short version of this walk, turn left, following a fingerpost for the Wetlands and Putney Bridge and walking with the river on your left and Harrods Village on your right. Continue along an attractive unsealed path, beneath the arms of weeping willows, poplar and sycamore trees (which conspire to hide the London Wetland Centre's lagoons on the right), and go past an obelisk and memorial to noted oarsman Steve Fairbairn, positioned exactly a mile from the Putney end of the Championship Course, to the junction where the Queen Elizabeth Walk joins from the right.

Alternatively, to do the full walk, turn right from Hammersmith Bridge and stroll along the Thames towards Barnes, with the river on your right and the enormous playing fields of St Paul's School, founded in 1509, on the left. Pass a large slipway and enter a green tunnel of beech, sycamore, ash and poplar trees. Across the water lies the tidal island of Chiswick Eyot, with the square tower of Chiswick's St Nicholas Church rising behind it. Mostly hidden by trees, Leg O' Mutton reservoir extends to your left. No longer used for drinking water, this large lake and surrounding meadowland was saved from development by residents, and is now a protected nature reserve providing habitat for myriad species of birds, bats and amphibians, including the great crested newt.

Emerge from the trees and walk along river-hugging Lonsdale Road into Barnes, passing the Bulls Head (a famous jazz venue) and The Waterman's Arms. If you've had enough, you can bail at Barnes Bridge Station (directly ahead, next to the railway bridge), otherwise turn left along Barnes High Street. Pass the Coach and Horses and The Sun Inn, and when the road splits around Barnes Green, bear left along Church Road to St Mary's Barnes, which boasts a 12th-century Norman tower. Walk through the church grounds and graveyard, passing the old Homestead Cottage. As you approach Byfeld Gardens, check out Olympic Studios on the left. Now operating primarily as a cinema, this building was once an illustrious recording studio used by artists including Ella Fitzgerald, BB King, Jimi Hendrix, David Bowie, the Beatles, the Rolling Stones, Led Zeppelin, Prince, Madonna, The Who, Adele and Björk.

Where Church Street meets Castelnau, cross at the lights to reach the Red Lion, then go straight ahead along Queen Elizabeth Walk, a tree-lined avenue leading to the WWT London Wetland Centre. Managed by the Wildfowl and Wetlands Trust, and constructed around four former reservoirs, this 40-hectare reserve is home to many rare riparian animals, including Asian small-clawed otters and a menagerie of waterfowl. There's an entrance fee, and you need half a day to explore properly, but it's worth diverting left for a flyby look.

Continue along the footpath running parallel to Queen Elizabeth Walk until you meet the Thames, and then turn right. Walk with the river and Craven Cottage stadium on your left, passing Barn Elms Boathouse on your right. Ignore a footpath leading right, cross a little bridge over Beverley Brook and go past Leader's Gardens.

Lined with London plane trees, several Alan Thornhill sculptures and umpteen rowing clubs, the Putney Towpath sends you along an extended slipway, past the Duke's Head and Putney Pier, to Putney High Street. Opposite St Mary's Church, mentioned in Samuel Pepys' diaries and Charles Dickens' *David Copperfield*, turn left and walk across Putney Bridge to the tube station (or go right for Putney station).

13

Brockwell Park and Brixton

Distance 3.5km **Time** 1 hour 30
Start Herne Hill ⇌
Finish Brixton ⊖ ⇌

This short stroll travels between two very different districts of London via Brockwell Park, a verdant expanse of playing fields, walled gardens and meadows, punctuated by ponds, populated by myriad species of birds, bats and butterflies, and crisscrossed by trails that transport you straight from urban streets into a bucolic setting which feels detached from the city, despite delivering eye-popping views of the Big Smoke's biggest buildings.

Emerge from Herne Hill station opposite The Commercial, a pub famed for its fantastic interior, and soak up the village-like atmosphere of the attractive south London suburb. Less than 10km from central London, Herne Hill remained distinctly rural until the railway arrived in 1862, facilitating easy travel into town and transforming the face of the place, as houses for the middle classes rapidly replaced working farmland.

Turn left and stroll along the pedestrianised Railton Road, passing bars, cafés, delis and boutiques. When you meet Dulwich Road, glance left to see the green Herne Hill sign painted on brickwork beneath the railway bridge in a drop-shadow sans-serif style widely imitated elsewhere. Bear right and cross the busy road at the lights, walking over one of a pair of permanent rainbow-coloured road crossings (the second one enlivens nearby Norwood Road in Tulse Hill).

Head towards the welcoming gates of Brockwell Park (open daily from 7.30am to 15 minutes before sunset). This 50-hectare park has hosted the London Pride festival twice, plus other progressive political and cultural happenings including the Rock Against Racism events in the late 1970s, a CND Festival for Peace in the 1980s, an Anti-Nazi League Carnival in the 1990s and 'Jayday' in the early 2000s, a pro-cannabis festival eventually cancelled because of suspicions about… drug use (true story). Besides the free Lambeth Country Show, large expos, gatherings, dance parties and concerts still happen here each summer, although they're usually ticketed, highly commercial events that take place behind fences, often amid criticism from local communities who continue to cherish and protect this great green space.

Walk straight up the hill towards Brockwell Hall, a large 19th-century house originally owned by a wealthy glass merchant. Local MP Thomas Lynn Bristowe led the movement that saw the hall and surrounding land being bought by the local council and transformed into a public park.

Tragically, Bristowe died of a heart attack on the steps of the house during the opening ceremony on 6 June 1892, but his legacy is commemorated with a bust displayed at Brockwell Hall. The building has undergone extensive renovations recently, but it usually offers café-style refreshments and facilities.

Stroll around the hall, keeping the building on your right and looking left to enjoy excellent views across the treetops and over the raised railway line to Dulwich Village and beyond. Occasional tree sculptures can be spotted across the grass, including one that resembles a dragon from afar. Wend right around the far end of the hall and walk past the impressive four-sided emerald-green standing clock known as the Tritton Tower, after the MP who succeeded Bristowe and donated the tall timepiece to the park to mark Queen Victoria's Diamond Jubilee in 1897.

Follow a fingerpost pointing towards the Walled Garden. While crossing the hill, look right for a fantastic vista of central London, with the Shard harassing the horizon as Brockwell Park's popular public lido sunbathes in the foreground (this outdoor pool offers wonderful respite from summer heat). To your left, across a meadow of wildflower-speckled grass and a copse of oak trees, the impressive spire of Tulse Hill's Holy Trinity Church points at the heavens. Runners and dog walkers are ever present, but on warm weekend days the park pulses with the rhythm of people picnicking, playing cricket, chasing their children and enjoying alfresco drinks with friends.

At the bottom of the hill, bear slightly right to discover a cute little community of miniature houses, the remnants of a more extensive bonsai-sized village designed and donated by retired engineer Edgar Wilson in 1947. Next to this diminutive delight, and beside a 200-year-old folly known as the Temple building, the Walled Garden is a little oasis of serenity, with flowerbeds and benches beautifully arranged around a central pond. In complete contrast to the boisterous parklife shenanigans outside, people come here to read, relax and decompress amongst aromatic herbs, plants and shrubs, all fastidiously attended to by bees and butterflies. (There's also a public toilet here, if nature calls in that way.)

Continue between the Walled Garden and a children's play area with a sandpit, paddling pool, water jets and stepping stones. Soon you meet

Brockwell Park Ponds, where stealthy herons stalk the banks and elegant swans share the water with coots and moorhens. Follow the path around the first pond, wending left and crossing a little wooden bridge, then turn right and walk alongside the second pond. The water might be mostly hidden behind foliage, but you'll often be treated to a cacophonous chorus of croaking from the charismatic common toads that live within. Keep strolling past a third pond, ignoring the next three right turns and the Tulse Hill and Arlingford Road park entrances on your left. Pass a bench (where you can be embraced by a big wooden toad) and arc right round an adventure playground before bearing left. Pass a colossal conker carving and exit Brockwell Park through Water Lane Gate.

Turn left along Brixton Water Lane, passing Arlingford Road and crossing Tulse Hill road at the lights. Continue and then, just past Rainsford House, turn right into Rush Common, a stretch of ribbon parkland with a woodland walk running along the right of Brixton Hill as you descend. The name Brixton apparently originates from 'Brixi's stone', a boundary marker placed atop this hill by a Saxon lord called Brixi, and this green corridor is a preserved strip of what was once, many centuries ago, a large commons area used for grazing sheep.

Pass Brixton Orchard (a community food-growing project) and cross St Matthew's Road, before ducking right into St Matthew's Church Gardens. Running along the route of an old river, Effra Road arrives from the right to meet Brixton Hill by the Budd Mausoleum, a monument built in 1825 that contains the remains of several members of a wealthy family. On your left is Electric Brixton (a live music venue and nightclub) and Lambeth Town Hall, but this route turns right and crosses Effra Road to enter Windrush Square.

Originally called Brixton Oval, and then Tate Gardens, this pedestrianised plaza was renamed in 1998, on the 50th anniversary of the arrival of the HMT *Empire Windrush*, to honour the contribution of the country's African

Caribbean community to British life and the Brixton area in particular. The Caribbean migrants aboard the *Windrush* and subsequent ships helped rebuild Blitz-battered London after WWII and filled gaping gaps in the workforce required to drive buses and trains, and provide nursing in the newly created NHS. Many settled here after initially being housed in appalling conditions in an old air raid shelter on Clapham Common, from where the nearest employment exchange was on Coldharbour Lane. The square features a memorial to African and Caribbean service personnel who fought for Britain in the World Wars.

Walk past the Tate Library, fronted by a bust of the 19th-century sugar-magnate Sir Henry Tate, who funded its foundation (along with other libraries and the Tate Gallery). Cross Coldharbour Lane by the Ritzy Cinema and continue along Brixton Road to arrive at Electric Avenue, leading right to Brixton Market. Dating to 1888, this was the first market street to be illuminated by electric lighting, but it's more famous to a generation for featuring in the title of a popular Eddy Grant song from 1983. Despite being very upbeat, *Electric Avenue* references the racially charged Brixton riots that had erupted two years earlier, amid deteriorating relationships between the police and local black youths who'd been repeatedly subjected to stop-and-search harassment.

From here, Brixton tube station is 25m down the road on the right, or continue for another 50m, then turn right along Atlantic Road to find Brixton railway station.

14

Blackheath to Greenwich

Distance 8km **Time** 3 hours
Start Blackheath ⇌
Finish North Greenwich ⊖

**Meander along the Prime
Meridian to the Millennium
Dome, travelling through time
across historical parkland and
past the Royal Observatory before
tracing the story-soaked shores
of the Thames to reach ultra-
modernised Greenwich Peninsula.**

Leave Blackheath station, turn left
and explore the café-lined streetscape
of beautiful Blackheath Village. Pass
Spencer Place to Tranquil Vale and cross
at the traffic island to go right along
Montpelier Vale. At the next fork, bear
left towards All Saints Church, crossing
Royal Parade and continuing along All
Saints Drive, keeping the church on your
right. The grassy area on the left was
historically used as a drying ground by
laundresses, and it retains the name
Washerwomen's Bottom.

Take the sealed path that crosses
Blackheath, going slightly right when it
splits, following a sign for Greenwich.

At Talbot Place, bear right towards
the tall trees. Glance east for views
of Severndroog Castle and Eltham.

In the Middle Ages, Blackheath saw
action during several insurrections.
Rebels rallied here before joining Wat
Tyler's 1381 Peasants' Revolt and Jack
Cade's Kentish Rebellion in 1450, and
the Battle of Deptford Bridge (also
called the Battle of Blackheath) in 1497
ended the First Cornish Rebellion, after
insurgents marched from the West
Country to London. In the 17th and
18th centuries, when highwaymen
haunted the wild heath, executed felons
were left hanging from gibbets on the
hill – a warning to would-be miscreants.

Go over the Millennium Circle, where
several paths intersect, straight towards
the busy road. Cross at the lights and
walk directly ahead along Duke
Humphrey Road to Charlton Way
(a London Marathon starting point).
Before going through the park gates
opposite, look right to see a plaque on
the wall inscribed in Cornish and
commemorating the 1497 rebellion.

In Greenwich Park, follow Bower

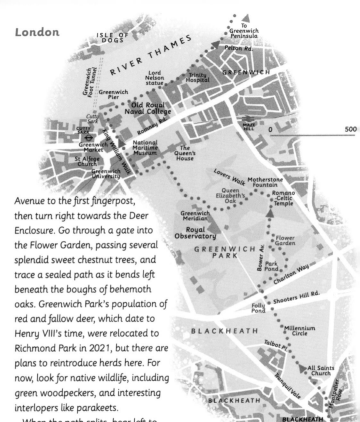

0   500

Avenue to the first fingerpost, then turn right towards the Deer Enclosure. Go through a gate into the Flower Garden, passing several splendid sweet chestnut trees, and trace a sealed path as it bends left beneath the boughs of behemoth oaks. Greenwich Park's population of red and fallow deer, which date to Henry VIII's time, were relocated to Richmond Park in 2021, but there are plans to reintroduce herds here. For now, look for native wildlife, including green woodpeckers, and interesting interlopers like parakeets.

When the path splits, bear left to walk with Greenwich Park Pond on your left, before going right and then left to leave the Flower Garden. Rejoin Bower Avenue, turn right and follow a fingerpost pointing towards the Roman Remains. At a confluence of paths, go straight ahead to see the site of a Romano-Celtic Temple, dating to circa 43–410AD. Turn left at the temple information board and walk along the 'no cycling' lane. Take the first left, by Motherstone Fountain, and ascend to Queen Elizabeth's Oak, the remains of a tree that stood here from the 12th century and features in tales about Henry VIII and his daughter Elizabeth I (both born in Greenwich Palace). Now horizontal and surrounded by railings, the oak was once big and hollow enough to be used as a prison.

At the next junction, go straight on, following fingerposts for the Old Royal Observatory, passing more sweet chestnuts before emerging in front of the galaxy-gazing building constructed for King Charles II in 1675 on a site selected by Christopher Wren. The planetarium is to your left, while on the right, overlooking all of London, is the General Wolfe Statue, commemorating the man credited with securing the colony of Canada for Britain after defeating the French in Quebec.

Astronomer Royal, Sir George Airy, drew a meridian line here in 1851 between the North and South Pole, via Greenwich, which was adopted as the planet's Prime Meridian in 1884, officially dividing the globe into eastern and western hemispheres (and further upsetting the French, who continued using the Paris Meridian on maps for decades). The time and date here at 0° longitude (Greenwich Mean Time or GMT) is the base for setting time zones around the world. The whole site is well worth exploring – there's an entry fee, but if you go through the gate by the Shepherd 24-hour Gate Clock, set in the main building wall, you can straddle the Prime Meridian Line for free.

After having a foot in each hemisphere, return to the clock and descend the steps and path beside the gate, enjoying an expansive vista over the Maritime Museum and *Cutty Sark*. At the bottom, go halfway round a set of small circular steps, then right along a wide beech-lined avenue leading to

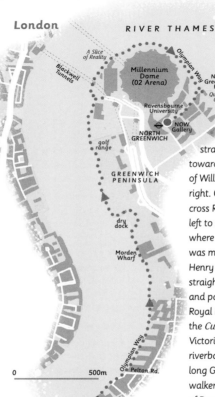

London

RIVER THAMES

A Slice of Reality

Blackwall Tunnels

Olympian Way

Millennium Dome (02 Arena)

North Greenwich Pier

Quantum Cloud

Cloud Cable Car

Ravensbourne University

NOW Gallery

NORTH GREENWICH

golf range

GREENWICH PENINSULA

dry dock

Morden Wharf

0 — 500m

Olympian Way

Pelton Rd.

Trinity Hospital

sculpture which spent two years on Trafalgar Square's Fourth Plinth. Leave Greenwich Park by St Mary's Gate and stroll straight along King William Walk towards the *Cutty Sark*, passing a statue of William IV (the 'Sailor King') on your right. Go past Greenwich University and cross Romney Road at the lights. Look left to see St Alfege Church – built where Alfege, Archbishop of Canterbury, was martyred by Vikings in 1012 and Henry VIII was baptised in 1491. Carry straight on, crossing College Approach and passing the entrance to the Old Royal Naval College courtyard, to reach the *Cutty Sark*. This record-breaking Victorian-era tea clipper resides on the riverbank by the entrance to the 370m-long Greenwich Foot Tunnel, which takes walkers beneath the Thames to the Isle of Dogs. If you've had enough, you can finish at the Cutty Sark DLR station or wander along Greenwich Church Street, passing St Alfege and Greenwich Market before taking Greenwich High Road to the main railway station. The full route, however, turns right along the Thames

the National Maritime Museum (free entry). Turn left and walk with the museum on your right, passing Yinka Shonibare's *Nelson's Ship in a Bottle*

Path to walk parallel to the Old Royal Naval College, passing an obelisk dedicated to Lieutenant Joseph-René Bellot of the French Navy, who perished during the search for Sir John Franklin's lost 1845 Arctic expedition. Low tides reveal sandy Greenwich Beach, but this isn't a place to play.

Round the corner to the Trafalgar Tavern, passing a statue of Nelson, and trace the tavern walls to walk along narrow Crane Street. Pass The Yacht pub and go along Highbridge Wharf, past 400-year-old Trinity Hospital. Continue along Crowleys Wharf, Anchor Iron Wharf and Ballast Quay, passing The Cutty Sark pub and embarking along Olympian Way. The surroundings get increasingly industrial, but a pier at Morden Wharf, where the path tiptoes between the beach and a brewery, offers excellent river views. After a dry dock, turn left and follow a fingerpost for 'North Greenwich station and Dome via riverside', rounding a concrete works and passing a golf driving range as the Millennium Dome pops into view.

The next section is enlivened by *The Line*, a series of art installations roughly tracing the Meridian Line. The first – Alex Chinneck's pylon-like *A Bullet from a Shooting Star* – is to your right. By a slipway, you can go right to reach North Greenwich tube, but this route follows the river around Greenwich Peninsula, passing what appears to be a road sign pointing along the Meridian and reading 'Here 24,859'; created by Jon Thomson and Alison Craighead, the number is the distance in miles to travel right around Earth. Keep going, past *A Slice of Reality* (a cross-section of a sand-dredger made by Richard Wilson) and Serge Attukwei Clottey's *Tribe and Tribulation*.

Continue circling the Dome, with the sky gondolas of the Cloud Cable Car high above your head. Pass Gary Hume's abstract *Liberty Grip* sculpture, and look right to spot *The Mermaid* by Damien Hirst. Turn right just before North Greenwich Pier, beyond which rises Antony Gormley's towering *Quantum Cloud*. Ascend steps, go under a walkway and pass the Ravensbourne University buildings and NOW Gallery to reach North Greenwich station in Peninsula Square.

Sydenham to One Tree Hill

Distance 5km **Time** 2 hours
Start Sydenham Hill ≈
Finish Honor Oak Park ≈

**This walk wanders through
ancient woodlands, past peculiar
follies hidden in foliage, and
pauses to explore an incredible
collection of curiosities before
continuing through parks,
gardens and graveyards to top
out at one of south London's best
viewing points on One Tree Hill.**

Leave leafy Sydenham Hill station via
the College Road exit, use the zebra
crossing and walk straight ahead along
a wide tree-fringed footpath. Pass a
board telling tales about local history,
including the story of The Crystal Palace,
which once glistened on the side of
Sydenham Hill 1km south of here. After
100m, turn left through a metal gate
into Dulwich Wood. Together with
Sydenham Hill Wood, this ancient mixed-
species treescape, managed by the
London Wildlife Trust, is a remnant of the
Great North Wood which swayed across
a huge swathe of south London for

centuries, supplying timber for myriad
local industries, including shipbuilding in
the Royal Naval dockyard in Deptford.

Stick to the main path, gently
ascending and passing a bench. At
a four-way junction with a bench, go
virtually straight ahead, taking the
path that bears slightly right. Keep
following this trail, lined with blooming
bluebells and wood anemone in spring,
as it wends through woods of oak,
beech, sycamore, hornbeam and holly.
Towards the end of the path, houses
appear through the branches on your
right. The path elbows left but go up a
small set of steps directly in front of you.

Cross a wide track (the route of the
long-extinct Nunhead–Crystal Palace
railway) and go straight ahead along a
sandy path that arcs left and brings you
to the intriguing mock-ruins of a 19th-
century folly. This enigmatic structure –
deliberately built to appear dilapidated
by antiquity – once stood in the gardens
of a Victorian villa belonging to David
Henry Stone, Lord Mayor of London in
1874. Other notable residents included
Lionel Logue, George VI's speech

therapist, but the flashy suburban mansions built here in the afterglow of The Crystal Palace's relocation nearby eventually all fell empty after the palace burned down. The last was demolished in the 1980s, the land was returned to nature (and the public) and the wild woods rapidly reclaimed the landscaped gardens, leaving the odd exotic cedar tree and occasional incongruous concrete curiosity as a faint echo of their presence.

From the folly and a wooden post marked with the number 4, keep going straight, ignoring a turning to the right. Stay on the well-formed path, disregarding the next two left turns. Pass a post inscribed with an 8, descend some steps and go through a metal gate. To your left, spanning the old railway line, is Cox's Walk Bridge, but this route turns right and climbs the steps. When the steps start steering right, by a pictorial board about Sydenham Hill Wood, turn left through a metal

gate and trace a gently descending path that eventually leads through Sydenham Hill housing estate. Follow waymarkers for the Green Chain Walk (GCW), a great web of trails linking green spaces across south London, which appear on wooden posts and lampposts.

Emerging from the estate, turn briefly right and use the traffic lights to go over Sydenham Hill road and then

Cambe
Old Cer

Wood Vale

Lordship Lane

bandstan

Horniman
Museum
& Gardens

London R

0   500m

Cox's
Walk
Bridge

Sydenham
Hill Wood

Dulwich
Wood

folly

College Rd

UPPER
SYDENHAM

SYDENHAM
HILL

across busy London Road. Pass through the gates opposite into Horniman Gardens, turn immediately right and walk along the path running parallel to the road, with the gardens sprawling to your left, until you reach the main park entry gates. Turn left here and stroll up to the Horniman Museum, a hidden gem packed full of wondrous artefacts and items of historical, ethnological, anthropological and botanical interest (including a colossal Canadian walrus, over-stuffed by well-meaning taxidermists unaware that live walruses are really wrinkly). There's a charge for the butterfly house, aquarium and some exhibitions, but the gardens and museum (housed in a stunning Art Nouveau building) are free to enter.

Keep ascending to the tarmac area around the bandstand, which boasts fantastic views across London and hosts a pop-up food market on Sundays. Pass the Sound and Musical gardens on your left. The Butterfly House is off to the right (along with a circular animal walk featuring goats, guinea pigs, sheep, rabbits, hens and alpacas), but this route continues straight past the bandstand. Trace the sealed path, arcing left around a hairpin bend, then go right, following green signposts and GCW arrows pointing towards Camberwell Old Cemetery and One Tree Hill. A second right turn takes you along an alleyway leading to Westwood Park. Emerge and turn left, following another GCW arrow, and then left again on Langton Rise.

At the mini roundabout, cross and then bear right to enter Camberwell Old Cemetery, last resting place of Frederick Horniman (tea trader and founder of the nearby museum) among other notables. Follow GCW pointers through the green graveyard, which has a memorial to 21 people killed in a WWI zeppelin raid on Camberwell, mostly keeping right each time the path forks. Exit the cemetery gates on Forest Hill Road by a GCW fingerpost pointing towards One Tree Hill and Peckham Rye Park. Turn right and walk up the hill.

Cross Forest Hill Road at the lights just before Wood Vale road, then turn left into Brenchley Gardens, following GCW arrows. Stroll through this attractive linear park, which incorporates the trackbed of the old Crystal Palace High Level Railway and features a sunken garden and flowerbeds that burst into colour during summer. Look left to glimpse good views of the city through sycamore and oak trees, across the greens of the Aquarius Golf Club ground which covers the top of Beechcroft Reservoir. Towards the end of the park, turn right and leave the gardens, following GCW arrows pointing towards Camberwell New Cemetery and crossing Brenchley Gardens road.

Ignore signage for the cemetery and walk straight ahead, following Green Chain Link (GCL) pointers through a gate opposite the pedestrian crossing, and take the rising path leading up One Tree Hill. Pass an information sign, ignore a right turn and continue uphill, climbing a couple of sets of steps beneath ash, oak, sycamore, blackthorn, poplar and London plane trees, listening out for woodpeckers and spotting warblers in summer and redwing, fieldfare and firecrest in winter.

For centuries this hill has been crowned by an 'oak of honor', originally a boundary tree planted on the seam between Kent and Surrey. Queen Elizabeth I apparently picnicked beneath its boughs on May Day 1602, while visiting Sir Richard Bulkeley; an amusing tangent to this tale claims the monarch got drunk and accidentally knighted the tree instead of the man, but sadly that's a whopping myth. Also embellished are stories about Dick Turpin hanging out here, but a local highwayman known as 'Brockley Jack' may well have preyed on potential victims from the hill, which once rose grand and green from the Great North Wood.

By the late 19th century its forested flanks were stripped bare, leaving the solitary oak looking lonely on the summit, hence the name One Tree Hill. Multiple trees have returned since the area became a nature reserve, but an 'oak of honor' remains close to the peak, ringed by railings. This oak, the third tree to be so ennobled, was planted in 1905 (when the park opened to the public) after its predecessor was struck by lightning in 1888.

Follow the sealed path as it arcs right, skirting around St Augustine Church, which lies part-hidden in a south-facing dip but was built atop the 90m-high hill in the late 19th century. Pass the GCL sign to reach the summit of One Tree Hill, and check out the view from the benches strategically arranged around the octagonal base of an old gun emplacement built here during WWI to protect the capital from aerial bombing by Germany's dreaded zeppelins and Gotha GV biplanes piloted by the Luftstreitkräfte. Such a violent threat is difficult to imagine on peaceful, clear days, when the city vista from the summit is superb.

Return to the GCL sign and follow the fingerpost pointing to St Augustine Church and Honor Oak station. Descend the path, passing the church on your left, and continue down steps to Honor Oak Road. Turn left and walk 200m to the station.

Richmond Park

Distance 14.5km **Time** 4–5 hours
Start & Finish Richmond ⊖ ≋

Sprawling across 1000 hectares of south London, Richmond Park is an easily accessible, great green escape area, full of wonderful wildlife and steeped in stories. It boasts a Bronze Age burial chamber and is famous for red and fallow deer, originally brought here in 1637 after Charles I relocated his entire court to nearby Richmond Palace, fleeing a plague that was ripping through London, and subsequently turned the surrounding terrain into a hunting park.

This park is one of Britain's best sites for spotting ancient trees, and some of the oaks that would have hidden the animals from the hunters 400 years ago are still alive today, dropping acorns that help sustain the current populations of deer through autumn and winter.

It's not just the deer that delight modern visitors to this richly diverse royal park. Richmond Park is London's largest Site of Special Scientific Interest, a National Nature Reserve and a European Special Area of Conservation, and it's home to an astonishing array of species – including birds, beetles, bats, insects, fungi, grasses and wildflowers – many of them quite rare.

To begin, leave Richmond railway station and turn left along The Quadrant. Pass the triangular Railway Tavern and, at The Square, continue straight ahead along George Street. At the end, opposite the Old Ship pub, bear left along Hill Street. Pass the turning that leads right, down to Richmond Bridge, and continue along Hill Rise. When the road forks keep left, ascending Hill Rise, which soon segues into Richmond Hill, passing the tiny Victoria Inn.

As you climb Richmond Hill, walk along the lower pathway on the right-hand side of the road, lined with benches. A stunning view along the River Thames soon opens up to your right, across Terrace and Buccleuch Gardens, a pair of pretty, tiered public parks built on the former grounds of three 18th- and 19th-century mansions (Buccleuch,

London

Landsdowne and Cardigan houses).

At the end of Terrace Gardens, pass the historic Nightwatchman's Hut (in place since 1887), and ascend steps to an open area overlooking the Thames, which skirts around Petersham Meadows far below. Richmond Bridge is to your right, and looking left along the river you can see Ham House, Strawberry Hill and Hampton Court.

Carry on past Wick House, then cross a mini roundabout featuring an ornate RSPCA monument built atop Collcutt Cattle Fountain. Pass the Royal Star and Garter Home, built to care for injured soldiers after WWI, and enter Richmond Park through Richmond Gate.

There are toilets on your right, but this walk turns left, passing a wildlife information board and a post with a waymarker for The Tamsin Trail, a 12km signed saunter around Richmond Park. Go straight on, strolling along a broad mixed-use track lined with maple and oak trees.

Pass Bishop's Gate on the left and Bishop's Pond on your right. When the track forks, stay right, walking on the wider path. Ignore another track leading right and keep going as the path undulates and twists. Cross a small bridge over a stream and continue with the park wall on your left. Beech, birch and oak trees, including some gnarly old specimens, stand

occasional flash of green as a parakeet darts between branches.

A Tamsin Trail waymarker directs you left towards Sheen Gate, but this route

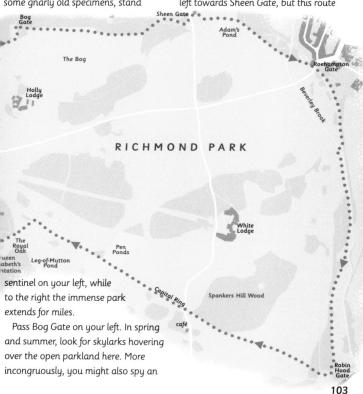

sentinel on your left, while to the right the immense park extends for miles.

Pass Bog Gate on your left. In spring and summer, look for skylarks hovering over the open parkland here. More incongruously, you might also spy an

continues straight to avoid the car park, before bearing left and crossing the sealed road around the gatehouse. On the other side of the road, take the path leading straight ahead, staying right when it forks and walking towards Adam's Pond.

Walk around the pond, with the water on your right, and keep going along the track, which soon widens. Cross a wooden bridge over Beverley Brook and continue past Roehampton Gate. Cross the road by the gate and follow a large fingerpost pointing towards Isabella Plantation, passing a café and cycle hire place. Continue along the path, with the golf course on your left and the road on your right. Cross Beverley Brook Bridge and keep tracing the track, following Tamsin Trail waymarkers and passing a milestone to Robin Hood Gate.

The wending, bending dirt path passes a fingerpost pointing left to Chohole Gate, but carry on. Just before reaching Robin Hood Gate, turn right through the small car park. Pass the park map, exit the car park, cross the road (looking out for bikes) and go up the gravel path. You are now on the Capital Ring trail.

At a crosspaths, go straight ahead. The gravel soon stops but keep going directly up the hill, across the grass and past a Capital Ring waymarker post, towards Spankers Hill Wood. A track joins from the right, but go straight on, with chestnut trees on your right.

Carry on, crossing the road by the car park and walking straight ahead along a broad clay track. Pass between Pen Ponds and keep going, walking uphill. Cross the sandy horse-riding track and climb for another 50m, until you see a Capital Ring waymarker post pointing left. Take this and walk towards the trees of Sidmouth Wood. Stick to the main trail, walking with the fence that circles the woodlands on your right and the oaks of Queen Elizabeth's Plantation on your left, including one wizened specimen known as The Royal Oak, thought to be around 750 years old.

Emerging from the trees, bear right and pick up a sealed-surface lane which leads across a sandy track to Queen's Road. Cross, go straight ahead over another track and, when you meet a Capital Ring fingerpost, follow the arm pointing towards Richmond Bridge,

escending some steps.
he path splays, but
eed the Capital Ring
rrows as they lead right,
ently uphill, before turning
ou left just below Pembroke
odge, a grand Georgian
nansion with tearooms, gardens
nd great Thames Valley views.

Descend past some magnificent cedar
rees and Henry's Mound, a prehistoric
urial chamber later used as a hunting
antage point by Henry VIII (who
llegedly waited here for confirmation
of Anne Boleyn's execution), now a top
spot for enjoying the legally protected
tree-framed view through the valley to
St Paul's Cathedral.

At the bottom, follow the Capital Ring
fingerpost pointing to Richmond Bridge
and leave the park via Petersham Gate.
Cross the road at the lights, then take
the footpath marked 'Capital Ring' on a
metal fingerpost by the bus stop
directly opposite the park exit, passing
between houses towards the Thames.

After St Peter's Church graveyard,
turn right along the lane and when this
elbows left, continue
straight ahead along the
Capital Ring. When you
reach Petersham
Meadows, walk
straight across on
the sealed path. Leave through
the gate at the far end and go
straight, passing a little café, to meet
the river. Turn right and go along the
Richmond Thames Towpath with the
water on your left, walking through
Buccleuch Gardens.

Pass a tunnel leading to Terrace
Gardens by an immense London plane
tree, but keep following the riverside
path towards Richmond Bridge, passing
pubs, restaurants and boat clubs, and
skirting Riverdale and Rotary Gardens.
Go under the bridge into another green
area, Richmond Riverside, where you'll
see a statue of modernist writer and
one-time local Virginia Woolf, sat with
a book on a bench.

To return to the station, turn right up
Water Lane, pass the Old Ship pub on
your left and retrace your footsteps
along George Street and The Quadrant.

Highgate to Crouch End

Distance 5.5km **Time** 2 hours 30
Start Archway ⊖
Finish Crouch End 🚋

**Leading from a leafy park
with sweeping views, around a
cemetery crowded with illustrious
dead and through an ancient
wildlife-rich woodland to Crouch
End, where cafés and bars abound,
this north London adventure is
an afternoon amble offering
quietude, curiosities and culture.**

Leave Archway tube via the Highgate
Hill and Whittington Hospital exit to
emerge in Navigator Square, named in
honour of the Irish navvies whose hard
graft built London's canals, railways and
underground tunnels. Many of these
men stayed in this corner of the capital,
raising families and leaving a Celtic
cultural legacy still evident in community
centres and bars. You won't find any
Irish theme pubs here – these are the real
deal. Pass one such institution, the
historic Hibernian high rise that is the
Archway Tavern (on your right), and
turn left up Highgate Hill. A San

Francisco-style cable tramway (Europe's
first) once ran up the hill between the
pub and Highgate Village, but it's long
gone, so continue on foot.

While you walk, look for Whittington's
Cat, a statue of the famous feline
companion of Dick Whittington, a
character based (extremely loosely) on
real-life Richard Whittington (1354–
1423), MP, several-time Lord Mayor of
London and philanthropist. According
to one version of the classic rags-to-
riches tale, a dejected young Dick
Whittington was shuffling up Highgate
Hill, intent on leaving London, when he
heard his fortune foretold in the pealing
of the Bow Bells, and promptly turned
around, made a mint (through the sale
and subsequent adventures of his cat)
and became mayor. The real
Whittington bequeathed a fortune to
improve London's medieval medical
institutions, and you soon pass
Whittington Hospital, titled in tribute to
his generosity. There's been a hospital
here since 1473, when St Anthony's
Chapel and Lazar House opened as a
home for lepers, but the Whittington was

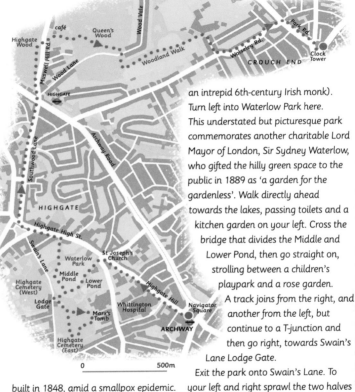

an intrepid 6th-century Irish monk). Turn left into Waterlow Park here. This understated but picturesque park commemorates another charitable Lord Mayor of London, Sir Sydney Waterlow, who gifted the hilly green space to the public in 1889 as 'a garden for the gardenless'. Walk directly ahead towards the lakes, passing toilets and a kitchen garden on your left. Cross the bridge that divides the Middle and Lower Pond, then go straight on, strolling between a children's playpark and a rose garden. A track joins from the right, and another from the left, but continue to a T-junction and then go right, towards Swain's Lane Lodge Gate.

Exit the park onto Swain's Lane. To your left and right sprawl the two halves of Highgate Cemetery, last resting place of an impressive list of eminent, illustrious and occasionally infamous folk, ranging from Karl Marx, George Eliot, Douglas

built in 1848, amid a smallpox epidemic.

Continue uphill, past a school, to green-domed St Joseph's Church, opposite Brendan the Navigator pub (named not for a navvy, but after

Adams, Malcolm McLaren and George Michael, through to Tom Sayers (a legendary bare-knuckle boxer whose bloody and brutal bouts sometimes stretched beyond 60 rounds) and Bruce Reynolds, who masterminded the 1963 Great Train Robbery. The remains of an estimated 170,000 people are buried in about 53,000 graves here, yet the cemetery seems spacious and leafy.

For the living there's an entry fee (£10 for both sides, £6 for just the east side, where Marx's impressive headstone can be found, along with the graves of Eliot, Adams, McLaren and many other familiar names). You can join guided tours (best booked ahead) to access famous features, including the Terrace Catacombs, Egyptian Avenue and the Circle of Lebanon. It's well worth exploring this north London necropolis for the often-extraordinary gravestones, occasional tongue-in-cheek tribute and brilliant (if sometimes unsettling) sculptures, including several that are dead ringers for Weeping Angels.

Leaving the cemetery, retrace your footsteps into Waterlow Park. Walk towards the ponds, but take the second left turn and ascend Lime Tree Avenue. Bear right at the fork by the Central Shelter, pass Upper Pond Nature Area on your left and climb to the top of the hilly park to exit through Highgate High Street Gate. Head left on Highgate High Street and cross the road at traffic lights by the Angel Inn. Continue uphill for another 100m, before turning right down Southwood Lane. Pass a blue plaque commemorating one-time resident Mary Kingsley (a pioneering Victorian-era explorer, ethnographer and writer) on your right and historic almshouses on the left. When the road forks, stay left and continue along Southwood Lane to Archway Road. Sharp-eyed fans of the RomZomCom classic *Shaun of the Dead* may recognise Liz's flat near the bottom of Southwood Lane, on Hillcrest off to the left.

Cross Archway Road at the lights, walking towards The Woodman pub. Highgate tube station is just to the right (if you've had enough), but this route goes straight ahead for 50m to the junction with Wood Lane, then crosses Muswell Hill Road at the lights. Continue downhill to a bus stop, then turn left through a gate into Highgate Wood. Follow the path leading right, walking parallel to the road, then take the first exit from the wood on the right. Cross Muswell Hill Road at the lights and enter Queen's Wood directly opposite.

Like Highgate Wood, Queen's Wood is a surviving section of the ancient Forest of Middlesex, which once covered London and its surrounds. Rumoured to have been used as a plague pit in the mid-17th century, this leafy haven is now a protected nature reserve. The wild wood has been largely left alone for centuries and consequently countless species of insects, birds and small mammals thrive beneath a canopy of towering English oak and beech trees, and amid myriad shrubs and smaller trees, including birch, rowan, cherry, field maple, hazel, holly, hornbeam, hawthorn, mountain ash and wild service. In spring, wood anemones and goldilocks boom into bloom and a tide of bluebells rises in the forest.

Trace the path past Queen's Wood Café. At the junction, turn right and stroll downhill. Pass a little pond on your right and an information board about the ancient bank enclosure (a 400-year-old boundary built to keep destructive deer and trespassers out) on your left. Meeting a fingerpost, go straight on, following the pointer for Queens Wood Road and Priory Gardens. Walk up the hill, climb some broad wooden steps and follow the path as it leans left and levels out. Bear right by a wooden post with a Capital Ring waymarker and cross the road. Re-enter Queens Wood on the other side and pick up the footpath leading straight ahead, following a large Capital Ring sign pointing into the trees.

The track descends through beech and holly and crosses another path. Look out for nuthatch and listen for the rat-a-tat of woodpeckers (green, great spotted and lesser spotted are all resident). In the early evening you might spy bats; the woods are home to several species, including soprano pipistrelles, natterer's and Daubenton's. Keep going straight, past a bench, then follow a wide path as it wends left and drops down a sequence of shallow steps. At the bottom, by a wall, leave the Capital Ring (which veers right, towards Priory Gardens) and go soft left (not sharp left, which leads uphill), and descend to a gateway in a metal fence. Pass through and amble along the Woodland Walk beneath beech, holly, sycamore, hawthorn and small oak trees, with allotments on your right.

Continue down two sets of shallow steps to a T-junction. Do a dogleg (left, then right) and pass through a metal gate. Turn immediately right and follow the path across a field as it traces the right touchline of a football pitch. At a T-junction by Highgate Wood School, turn right and emerge on Montenotte Road. Walk 100m along this suburban street to the junction with Shepherds Hill/Wolseley Road, then turn left. When you meet Park Road, head right and walk through the vibrant strip of shops and cafés to Crouch End clocktower. With a village vibe and numerous bars, bakeries, bookshops and bistros, Crouch End is popular with creatives, comedians, actors and artists (David Tennant, Simon Pegg, Katherine Ryan and Alan Carr all live locally, as did Sean Hughes, now sadly missed). The central clocktower, designed by the architect Frederick Knight, is a memorial to much-loved local leader Henry Reader Williams, who campaigned consistently for improved welfare for children and led the battles to save Highgate Woods and Queen's Wood when the threat of rapacious development hung over the treescapes in the 1880s.

18

Hampstead Heath

Distance 8km **Time** 3 hours
Start & Finish Hampstead Heath ⇌

From London's most famous open-air swimming ponds to the top of Parliament Hill, where kites cavort above sensational city views, this Hampstead hike explores a heathland resonant with history and wildlife, rich in legend and literary connections, and haunted by tales of highwaymen and duelling gents.

Leave Hampstead Heath station and cross South Hill Park Road. On your right is the Magdala Tavern, where Ruth Ellis – the last woman to be hanged in Britain – fatally shot her lover, David Blakely, in 1955. The tree-lined path opposite the station snakes right and climbs slightly as it enters the heath. Stroll past benches overlooking the imaginatively named Hampstead Ponds No 1 and No 2, which ripple on your right as moorhens, coots and swans disturb the surface. Statuesque herons hunt along the banks beneath trees populated by ring-necked parakeets – part of a garrulous green population that now enliven several London parks.

When the track forks, bear right and cross between Hampstead No 2 Pond and the Mixed Bathing Pond. Turn left and wander up an unsealed path. Before the swimmers' entry point (open to the public May–October, fee payable) follow the path right, away from the water. Ascend shallow steps, then turn left along a sealed path and walk past a mighty oak in an area busy with squabbling squirrels. About 200m to the right lies the enigmatic Hampstead Heath Tumulus, a mysterious mound surrounded by myths (many involving Queen Boudica and prehistoric battles) which is possibly a Bronze Age burial site.

Look out for muntjac deer as you pass a large green space with an undercover picnic area on your right. At the green's end, by a drinking fountain, cross Lime Avenue. Continue straight on along a track that broadens and then crosses Viaduct Bridge. This ornate pond-spanning structure dates to the mid-19th century when Sir Thomas Maryon Wilson, lord of the manor of Hampstead, attempted to monetise his heathland landholdings by building salubrious villas. The controversial development drew ire from locals and other Londoners (including Charles Dickens), and his plan was thwarted, but not before the ornamental pond and viaduct had been built.

Continue along the broad track. Bird Bridge (another feature of Wilson's ill-fated plan) is off to the right, but carry straight on, walking uphill and passing toilets and a drinking fountain, until a green area (site of an old fairground) opens up to your right. To the left lies the Vale of Health, one-time home of D H Lawrence (the *Lady Chatterley's Lover* author later penned a short unsettling Hampstead Heath-based horror story called *The Last Laugh* – best left unread if you're planning an after-dusk visit), but this route continues straight.

Meeting Spaniards Road, turn left and walk 50m to a pedestrian crossing by a roundabout. Cross the road, skirt around the Hampstead War Memorial and continue across North End Way to Jack Straw's Castle, named after a leader of the 1381 Peasants' Revolt, who was

allegedly captured and executed here. Jack Straw's Castle – claimed to be London's highest pub – served beer here for centuries, to Dickens and William Makepeace Thackeray among others. The pub, which features in Bram Stoker's *Dracula*, shut in 2002, but the building still bears the name.

Turn right along North End Way, cross Heath Brow, continue for 50m, then go left along a track into trees just before Inverforth House. After 75m you'll see an entrance to the Hill Garden and Pergola on your right. This hidden gem was commissioned by soap tycoon Lord Leverhulme in 1904 to beautify his mansion, Inverforth House, and is now maintained and kept open to the public (during daylight hours) by the City of London. Venture in, climb the spiral steps and wander along the wisteria-covered zigzagging length of the cupola-crowned pergola, an ornate raised walkway festooned with seasonal flowers and

entwined with vines, which offers excellent views over West Heath. At the end, descend into a garden arranged around a rectangular pond. Walk past the water feature, take the path going left and then turn right at the next junction and walk slightly uphill to an exit gate. Leave the gardens, turn left and follow the track. At a main junction, go right. (To skip the gardens, continue past the entrance, bear right and walk along the track with the pergola on your right. At a fork, stay left. Ignore a path that intersects yours and keep following the main track. At the next fork – where those exiting the pergola rejoin this path – bear left.)

Follow the main track, cross Sandy Road and go through gates into Golders Hill Park. Head straight towards a cube-shaped modern art installation, passing a deer enclosure on your left, beyond which is a free zoo with animals including Madagascan ring-tailed lemurs, Scottish wildcats, a Eurasian eagle-owl, and wallabies and kookaburras from Australia. Keep the bandstand on your right and head towards the bird pond. At the water's edge, turn briefly right and then left to cross a little bridge. Pass the butterfly house and a walled garden on your left, cross a wooden bridge on the right and head on past the insouciant *Golders Hill Girl* statue.

Continue past toilets and a café, leave the park and turn right along North End Way. Use the pedestrian crossing by the Old Bull and Bush pub, then turn left along North End. Pass Parfitt Close and Wildwood Terrace and re-enter the tree-covered heath. Go straight (slightly right) up the gentle slope, ignoring other paths. Pass a shallow pond on your right and continue until you exit the woods and emerge on Spaniards Road.

Use the zebra crossing, turn left and walk 50m to the old Toll House (dating to 1710) and the splendid Spaniards Inn, a tale-drenched tavern built in 1585 by two Spanish brothers (according to legend, at least), which became a hangout for hoods preying on London-bound travellers. Notorious highwayman Dick Turpin certainly spent time here, since his dad was the landlord for a while. The pub was also famously frequented by poets, including Lord Byron and John Keats (who apparently wrote 'Ode to a Nightingale' in the beer garden), and it features in Dickens' *Pickwick Papers* and Bram Stoker's *Dracula*.

Continue along Spaniards Road, passing Kenwood House on your right. This 17th-century mansion, home to the Earls of Mansfield for centuries, narrowly escaped destruction during the 1780 Gordon Riots when the Spaniards Inn landlord distracted the mob with free ale until the cavalry arrived. Later it was bought by Lord Iveagh (of the Guinness brewing dynasty), who left it to the nation in 1927. Packed full of art – including works by Rembrandt and Turner, and with sculptures by Barbara

Hepworth, Henry Moore and Eugène Dodeigne in the gardens – it's now maintained by English Heritage and open to the public (entrance fee for non-members). Just past the estate's second gate, a park entrance returns you to Hampstead Heath.

Stroll straight, following the main track around Prospect Hill. Central London emerges ahead, while Beechwood House, St Michael's spire and Highgate Hill dominate the view left. Follow the sealed path as it bears left around the perimeter of Kenwood Gardens. After passing Stock Pond on your right, turn right and walk uphill along a sealed path towards the Duelling Grounds, where scores were settled and insults avenged in the 18th and 19th centuries.

At a junction beside a gate into Kenwood Gardens, turn left along a sealed path. Walk downhill, with Kenwood Ladies' Bathing Pond off to your left, until you meet Highgate Ponds. Turn right along the edge of the Model Boating Pond. At a confluence of paths, go straight over and walk with the Men's Bathing Pond on your left.

Pass Highgate No 1 Pond and when the track splits three ways, go right, ascending Parliament Hill via a sealed path. At a fork, bear right and climb to the summit to enjoy superb city views – a particularly fantastic sight as day segues into night and London's lights start to twinkle. Continue over the brow of the hill. At the next main junction, turn left and walk until you meet Parliament Hill road. Carry on down the pavement (past a plaque on the second house on the right, where George Orwell once lived) until you pass the Magdala and reach the station.

19

Kingston to Kew

Distance 14.5km **Time** 4–5 hours
Start Kingston ≈
Finish Kew Bridge ≈

Tracing the Thames as London's majestic waterway wends through the most scenic sections of the city, this is one of the world's best riparian rambles. Rowers skim along the river while walkers amble along the banks, past palaces, parkland, gardens and locks. It's long, but there isn't a single hill and you can cut the route in half and do it in two stages by stopping at Richmond.

Exit Kingston station, cross Wood Street at the lights and stroll straight ahead along Fife Road. Take the first left along pedestrianised Castle Street and, at the junction, turn right along car-free Clarence Street. Pass All Saints Church, cross Thames Street and descend the ramp to the riverside, just left of Kingston Bridge. Turn right along the Thames Path, following fingerposts pointing towards Teddington Lock and walking along the Surrey side of the river, going under one of the five arches of the historic bridge which dates to 1828, although there's been a crossing here for centuries.

Pass Turks Pier and boatyard, go under a railway bridge and enter leafy Canbury Gardens, walking beneath soaring London plane trees. On the opposite bank, swanky houses have gardens extending right down to the river, many boasting boathouses. Keep wandering beside weeping willows dangling their languid limbs in the water and past a bandstand. Look left to see Steven's Eyot, a small tree-covered islet named after the boatman who had a cottage here, where the Boaters Inn now stands.

Pass Kingston Rowing Club, leave the lovely park and continue along Lower Ham Road; a raised footpath runs to the right of the riverside road from Albany Boathouse. Go past Albany Outdoors/ Sea Scout hut on your right and Tamesis sailing club on the opposite bank. Paddlers and dinghy sailors are often out on the water here. Shortly you reach Half Mile Tree where an elm tree stood, half a mile from Kingston, for centuries, becoming a local landmark and appearing on Ordnance Survey maps; when it died the trunk was filled with concrete, but it was eventually replaced by a horse chestnut in 1952. Leave Lower Ham Road here and stroll along the track running next to the river, which quickly forks into a footpath and a cycleway.

After 1km you go beneath an impressive footbridge and reach Teddington Lock, a complex of three locks and a weir spanning the Thames via two islands. It's worth crossing to the upper island (via the lock gates or footbridge) to explore the lock-keeper's cottage and attractive bridge leading to the opposite bank. The weir here marks the tidal limit of the Thames, so beyond this point (in the direction you're walking, towards central London), the water rises and falls twice daily. In 1940, a flotilla of boats assembled at the lock before departing to take part in the vacuation of Allied troops from Dunkirk. Return to the Surrey bank and keep racing the Thames Path as the riverside rail tiptoes under the shade of sycamore, elder, oak and ash trees, and the retreating tide reveals small stony beaches where waders and even brave bathers take to the water in summer. Just past the Teddington Obelisk, the path opens up and suddenly there's water on both sides, with the Thames Young Mariners lagoon on your right, used by youth and community groups for watersports and outdoor pursuits.

Pass through a verdant tunnel of hawthorn and oak to continue through Ham Lands Local Nature Reserve. Eel Pie Island – named after pies sold in an historic inn that once occupied the bit – appears on your left. The island later had a hotel and live music venue that saw performances from big bands, including The Rolling Stones, The Who and Pink Floyd. In the 1970s it hosted a huge hippie commune, but is now mostly occupied by artists in private residences, although the public are invited in periodically to peruse and purchase their work.

After passing a car park and jetty, look right to spot Ham House, hiding in the trees. Managed by the National Trust, this art-crammed 17th-century Stuart mansion and its gardens are worth exploring properly, but for a quick look turn right and approach the gates. Take in the house, then go left and walk along the unsealed path beside the property, before turning left along another track and walking with horse paddocks on your right. Cross a little wooden bridge and return to the riverside, emerging by the Hammerton's Ferry stop, which shuttles paying punters to Twickenham on the far bank.

Continue along the Thames Path, following fingerposts for Richmond and Kew Bridges. Look left across the water for views of Marble Hill House, a grand Neo-Palladian villa built for Henrietta Howard, mistress of King George II, which starred in the film *Interview With a Vampire*. Pass a fingerpost offering an alternate route in case of flooding, but continue straight if possible, passing Petersham Woods on your right, fronted by colossal conker trees. An ait appears in the river and the woods give way to

Map labels:
To Kew · Petersham Meadows · Marble Hill House · RIVER THAMES · Thames Path · TWICKENHAM · Eel Pie Island · Ham House · 0 500m · Ham Lake · Young Mariners · STRAWBERRY HILL · Ham Lands Local Nature Reserve · obelisk · TEDDINGTON · Teddington Lock

briefly, before entering Buccleuch Gardens through a kissing gate. Wildflowers and a magnificent horse chestnut frame a view of Richmond Bridge from this green oasis. Pass Richmond Canoe Club, a Rick Stein restaurant and boat moorings, before strolling through Midhurst Site and along Mears Walk towards the elegant arches of 18th-century Richmond Bridge. Go under, and then look right to see a bronze sculpture of Virginia Woolf sitting on a bench – the modernist author lived in Richmond and set up Hogarth Press here. Signs about seals appear around St Helena Pier, opposite Corporation Island, where – incredibly – the inquisitive aquatic mammals have been seen in recent years.

From the White Cross pub, walk along cobbles and past arches, home to

Petersham Meadows, majestically overlooked by Petersham and Richmond Hill Hotels on Richmond Hill.

Follow the path away from the river

pottery and coffee outlets. At the corner, continue on Cholmondeley Walk, passing a couple of small islands. After going under the railway and ducking beneath Twickenham Bridge, the Old Deer Park sprawls to your right; originally a royal hunting park established by James I in 1604, this grassy green expanse now offers breathing space and sporting facilities to the public.

Pass Richmond Lock and Weir, the last lock on the river's route to the sea. The footbridge here offers excellent views along the Thames (and a free water-bottle refill station), but return to the Richmond bank to enjoy a leafy section of the Kew Riverside Walk, strolling between a stream and the river, observing hunting herons, dancing dragonflies and fluttery butterflies. Benches offer views across the water to tree-covered Isleworth Ait and the 14th-century tower of All Saints church in the attractive riverside hamlet of Isleworth – once home to Vincent van Gogh and J M W Turner. By a sign for the Old Deer Park, look right, through the trees, to spot an obelisk, and beyond that – across Royal Mid-Surrey Golf Course – the King's Observatory, commissioned in 1769 by curious King George III.

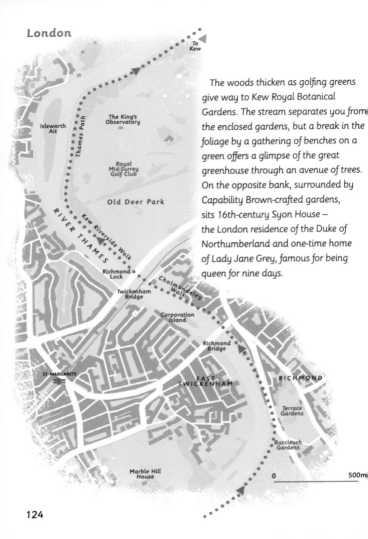

The woods thicken as golfing greens give way to Kew Royal Botanical Gardens. The stream separates you from the enclosed gardens, but a break in the foliage by a gathering of benches on a green offers a glimpse of the great greenhouse through an avenue of trees. On the opposite bank, surrounded by Capability Brown-crafted gardens, sits 16th-century Syon House – the London residence of the Duke of Northumberland and one-time home of Lady Jane Grey, famous for being queen for nine days.

Continue along the path, beneath beech and lime trees. Spot Simon Packard's controversial *Liquidity* sculpture on the far bank, opposite Kew Gardens' car park and entry. To your right, as you pass Lot's Ait and Brentford Ait, is Kew Palace, built in 1631 for wealthy silk merchant Samuel Fortrey and used as a royal residence during the Georgian period.

Just before Kew Bridge, turn right, following fingerposts for Kew Gardens, and then ascend steps, picking up signage for Kew Bridge station.

Wander over the wide-span bridge, cross the busy junction at the lights, turn right at the Express Tavern and find the station beside the Brentford FC Community Stadium.

Wimbledon Common and Putney Heath

Distance 6km **Time** 2 hours
Start Wimbledon ⊖ ⇌
Finish Wimbledon Park ⊖

Bouncing from the atmospheric cafés and watering holes of Wimbledon Village into the green expanse of the Wimbledon and Putney Commons – past ponds, through mixed woodlands, over a hill crowned by a landmark windmill and across a corner of London's largest heath – this walk serves up surprises and aces aplenty, before passing the world's most famous tennis club to arrive at Wimbledon Park.

A semi-wild wonderland beloved by local walkers, families, runners and riders, the commons were saved from enclosure by a landmark public access ruling in 1871, after Earl Spencer, lord of Wimbledon Manor, tried to fence the whole place off for his own profit. While exploring, look skyward to spy birds of prey, including kestrels, sparrowhawks, hobby and buzzards. Sadly, you're unlikely to spot any wombles while wandering – Wimbledon's favourite fictional inhabitants, lovable litter-picking eco-pioneers of the recycling revolution, are as good as extinct now – but if you're still out around dusk, you might see foxes, badgers and bats, and hear tawny owls hooting.

Leave Wimbledon railway station and turn right. Cross Alexandra Road at the lights and wander straight up Wimbledon Hill Road, past the Hand and Racquet pub. Keep walking along the ascending tree-lined path until you pass a working water fountain and reach Wimbledon Village. There are cafés and bistros aplenty here, and it's the perfect people-watching spot to pause for breakfast, lunch or coffee.

Cross Belvedere Grove and keep going straight, past an old cattle trough now filled with flowers. At the roundabout by the Dog and Fox Hotel, bear left along High Street, following a fingerpost pointing towards Wimbledon Common. You soon reach the Rose and Crown, one of Wimbledon's oldest pubs, which

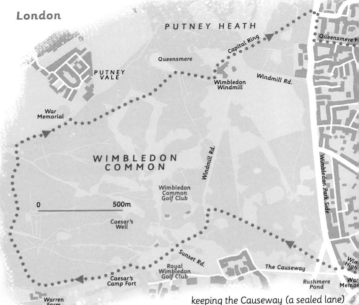

PUTNEY HEATH

Queensmere Po...

Capital Ring

Queensmere

Windmill Rd.

Wimbledon
Windmill

PUTNEY
VALE

War
Memorial

Wimbledon Park Side

Windmill Rd.

WIMBLEDON
COMMON

0   500m

Wimbledon
Common
Golf Club

Caesar's
Well

Sunset Rd.

Win...
High...

Royal
Wimbledon
Golf Club

The Causeway

Caesar's
Camp Fort

Rushmere
Pond

War
Memor...

Warren
Farm

dates to the mid-17th century and was regularly patronised (albeit at different times, despite the misleading sign outside) by the Victorian poets Leigh Hunt (who was once jailed for insulting George IV when he was Prince Regent) and boozy rabble-rouser Algernon Swinburne.

Continue towards the tall cross-topped Wimbledon War Memorial. Cross the road (The Green) to the grassy common,

keeping the Causeway (a sealed lane) on your left. Walk straight ahead along the dirt track directly opposite the memorial, crossing bridlepaths churned-up by horses and passing several London plane trees. Rushmere Pond is over to your left, beyond the Causeway. Cross a small sealed lane (Cannizaro Road) and keep going straight ahead along the path. Enter mixed woodlands of beech, birch, hawthorn, holly and fir, and walk along a wide track, with a ditch on your right and another track running parallel

Wimbledon Common and Putney Heath

left here and follow the main path, which runs parallel to a track known as Windmill Road. Ignore a path coming in from the left and keep alert for flying balls as you cross part of Wimbledon Common Golf Course. When the track forks, after about 400m, stay left and cross a sealed lane (Sunset Road). Continue along the track on the other side, passing more golfing greens before the path enters woods and wends right, joining another track.

Bear right on this wide track. Beyond the fence on your left lie the remains of confusingly-named Caesar's Camp Fort, a circular earthen structure built by a Celtic Iron Age tribe several hundred years before the Romans rocked up in Britain – although Emperor Claudius' legions likely stormed the place when they invaded in 43AD; sadly it's now mostly covered by Royal Wimbledon Golf Course (a public right of way crosses the site, but you can't access it from this route).

Ignore scrappy paths leading off left and right but, when you reach a distinct

to your path. Scratchy tracks and small trails lead off left and right, but stick to the main path which arcs around a more open area with benches.

At a knotted confluence of paths and trails, keep going straight ahead until you reach an obvious cross-tracks. Turn

fork, with Warren Farm on your left, bear right and descend gently through trees. Keep on the main track, ignoring a left turn and subsequent smaller paths. Cross a small stream and, at a junction, keep going straight on, over another stream. Continue across a second intersection and, when a third track crosses your path in an 'S' shape around a small triangle of grass, go directly ahead again. A few strides later you meet a post with a Capital Ring waymarker; bear right here to walk a section of this 125km long-distance London-ringing route, strolling through trees with sports fields on your left and mixed woodlands on the right.

At a T-junction a path leads left to a WWI memorial, but this route goes right and then immediately left, following Capital Ring signage to hike uphill through trees. Keep following Capital Ring arrows across a few more fairways as the path undulates and then descends into Putney Vale to meet Queensmere Pond, the deepest of the nine meres (lakes) that ripple across Wimbledon and Putney Commons. Prior to the pond being created (to commemorate Queen

Victoria's Diamond Jubilee in 1897) this was a famous duelling spot, until a man was fatally shot in 1838 and the violent quarrel-settling practice was prohibited. When you meet the water's edge, which is fringed with a mix of mature trees, follow Capital Ring waymarkers as they direct you right, up the hill.

At the top, follow signs towards the windmill, passing the London Scottish Golf Clubhouse, the Windmill Tearoom and a museum that explains the history of windmills in general and tells the story of this particular one, which was built here in 1817. Walk almost entirely around the four-sailed structure, until you're standing with the car park on your left and the windmill on your right.

To the north (left) sprawls Putney Heath, where highwaymen once prowled and duels were fought – including the infamous 1809 exchange between cabinet ministers George Canning and Lord Castlereagh, during which both men survived being hit by bullets. In 1795, Jeremiah 'Jerry' Abershaw, a notorious highwayman, was caught in the Green Man pub on the heath's northern edge (near the

Wimbledon Common and Putney Heath

birthplace of Thomas Cromwell, Henry VIII's chief minister); after his execution, Abershaw's body was hung in a gibbet on a rise now known as Jerry's Hill, off to your left.

Cross the road and stroll across the green, following a fingerpost pointing towards Wimbledon Park. More Capital Ring signs lead you through woodlands to Wimbledon Parkside (a road). Cross at the lights and go right, walking along the pavement past the Wimbledon Synagogue. At the bus stop you can catch bus 93, which takes you back to Wimbledon Village, but this walk turns left along Queensmere Road.

Keep following Capital Ring signage through the sleepy suburban streetscape of southwest London, and turn left along Bathgate Road. When you meet Church Road, you can quickly divert right to see the legendary courts of the All England Lawn Tennis and Croquet Club, known to tennis fans around the world simply as 'Wimbledon' and regarded as the home of lawn tennis (the version of the sport played on grass). It's only a five-minute walk each way, but this route crosses the road at the traffic islands and goes left, following Capital Ring waymarkers.

Walk with Wimbledon Park on your right. At the end of the fence, follow a sign for Wimbledon Park tube station and turn right into the park, a recreational green space that sprawls across 67 acres. Once you're in the park, turn right and walk along a sealed path with a fence on your right. Zigzag around an athletics ground (partially hidden behind tall fir trees) to reach Wimbledon Park Lake, and then walk with the water on your right. Continue past a children's playground and yet more tennis courts, climb the steps by the Metropolitan Police office, go through the park gates and turn left along Home Park Road. Turn left on Arthur Road, and Wimbledon Park Station is 50m down the street on your right.

Crystal Palace Park and Dulwich Common

Distance 8.5km **Time** 3 hours
Start Crystal Palace ⇌
Finish West Dulwich ⇌

After an eccentric start amid a monstrous menagerie of delightfully dated dinosaurs, this walk explores a section of the Green Chain Walk, joining the dots between several leafy oases that punctuate south London and offer blessed relief from the streetscape, with ancient woodlands and peaceful ponds.

Crystal Palace takes its name from a vast glass, wood and iron structure created to house the 1851 Great Exhibition in Hyde Park, which was subsequently dismantled, moved and rebuilt on the side of Sydenham Hill. The building burned down in 1936 and all that remains is a museum to tell the story, a single cast-iron column from the original structure that stands nearby (just left of where this walk starts) and a collection of curious creatures.

Exit Crystal Palace station and turn right, following signs for the Green Chain Walk (GCW), a web of trails connecting parks across south London. As you approach Crystal Palace Park, a towering mast punctures the sky; this is the Crystal Palace transmitter, the tip of which is more than 330m above sea level (higher than the top of the Shard). Don't cross the road; instead go right and stroll along a gravel track, following Capital Ring and GCW signage pointing towards the Dinosaur Park, information centre and café.

Pass the National Sports Centre (occupying a site where the FA Cup Final was played annually between 1895 and 1914) on your left and Crystal Palace Park farm (right). When the track becomes sealed and then forks by Capel Manor College, go slightly right and then straight ahead towards the giant head of a hylaeosaurus (a dinosaur). Reaching Lower Lake, turn left and walk around the ornamental pond with the water on your right, passing more monsters, including a mosasaur, pterodactyl, megalosaurus and teleosaurus.

Commissioned to accompany The Crystal Palace when it arrived, and created by Benjamin Waterhouse Hawkins, these fantastic beasts were the world's first dinosaur sculptures when they were unveiled in 1854, but they're wildly inaccurate according to modern palaeontologists.

Turn right, cross the wooden bridge, then bear right and amble along the lakeside with the water on your right. Turn right over another bridge, then go left, walking with water on both sides of the path and pedalos on the lake to your right. Keep going, past an Irish elk, to the boathouse, then bear right, following Capital Ring and GCW arrows. When you see the café on your left, leave the lake and descend towards it, passing Guy the Gorilla. Pop in or go past the café and toilets, and continue straight ahead across the grass (if it's muddy, turn left and then right to walk along the gravel track on the far side of the children's play area). Join the gravel track by the Memorial Bell.

At the T-junction, turn left, following a Capital Ring arrow. When the skatepark appears on your left, turn right up the hill, then bear left to walk with the fishing lake on your right. Keep going straight, slightly uphill, passing a maze on your left and heading towards the massive mast (toe-to-top London's eighth tallest structure, which beams TV into homes across the capital). At the green signpost, turn right, following the GCW. When the wide path bends right and forks, choose the smaller path leading left, then take the next right.

Exit the park through Westwood Hill Gate and turn right. Cross Crystal Palace Park Road at the lights and go straight, walking downhill along Westwood Road, following GCW pointers for Sydenham Hill Wood and Horniman Gardens along the 'Route avoiding steps'. By the bus stop opposite Charleville Circus, turn left down steps and walk along Ormanton Road. Cross Longton Avenue and go through a gate into Sydenham Wells Park. Follow GCW arrows through the peaceful park, named after

medicinal springs discovered here in the 1600s, crossing the pond and passing several unusual trees, including dawn redwood.

Exit the park and turn left up Wells Park Road. At the top, go over Sydenham Hill road at the zebra crossing and continue straight along Crescent Wood Road. Opposite Wood House, a lane leads left to Sydenham Hill station, but this route continues around the crescent, passing two entrances into private Peckarmans Wood. Immediately after the second, follow a GCW fingerpost through a gate into Sydenham Hill Wood. With adjacent Dulwich Wood, this leafy refuge is a surviving remnant of the Great North Wood that once covered south London from Croydon to New Cross, supplying fuel for furnaces and forges, timber for shipbuilding and resources for locals.

The path plunges through mixed woods, going down two sets of steps to meet a broad lane, which is the old trackbed of the

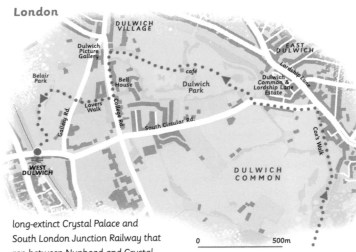

long-extinct Crystal Palace and South London Junction Railway that ran between Nunhead and Crystal Palace. To the right the track disappears into a tunnel (now a bat cave), but this walk turns left and traces the ghost railway route, beneath the boughs of oak, beech, sycamore, holly and hornbeam. In spring a tide of flowering bluebells flows around the ankles of the trees, flecked with white wood anemone, wild garlic and woodruff. Look for birds, including black caps, firecrest, nuthatch, green and great spotted woodpeckers, jay and tiny treecreepers.

At the end of the walkable section of the track, arrows lead you left, then right. Exit the woods through a metal gate, ignore Cox's Bridge spanning the old railway line on your right and walk straight ahead, following GCW signage for Dulwich Park via Cox's Walk. Built by a local publican in the 1730s to encourage people to visit the long-gone Green Man tavern on Dulwich Common, this oak-lined avenue now provides a thoroughfare for hikers and hedgehogs.

Pass a golf course and cricket pitch, and at the end of Cox's Walk go through a gate and turn left along the South Circular Road, following GCW signage. Cross at a traffic island just past 'Lordship Lane and Dulwich Common

Estate', continue for 50m and then, opposite sports fields, turn right through Rosebery Gate into Dulwich Park, an attractive Victorian-era oasis with a boating pond. Pass a pretty house on your left, fronted by the Dulwich Vegetable Garden community project. Go left on Carriage Drive, then bear right to walk through the American Garden, populated by plants from the east coast of the United States and resplendent with flowering rhododendrons in May.

Continue west through the leafy park, past a children's playground and a mural of three boys by street artist STIK, part of the Dulwich Outdoor Gallery, a series of open-air artworks around south London, many inspired by the Dulwich Picture Gallery's Old Masters. Pass the Dulwich Clock Café and a boating lake on your left, following signs for Dulwich Village. Exit College Gate via Carriage Drive and use the zebra crossing on College Road. Dulwich Village is right, but this route goes left, following the GCW Link route to West Dulwich station.

Pass (or pause to peruse) the Dulwich Picture Gallery, which opened in 1817 with an impressive collection of European Old Masters, and purports to be the planet's first purpose-built public art gallery. Pay to enter the beautiful John Soane-designed building (the lantern roof in the mausoleum inspired the look of Britain's iconic red phoneboxes) or explore the three-acre garden and grounds, where Japanese maple and Kentucky coffee tree grow (free entry).

Continue along College Road, passing Bell House (historic home to numerous luminaries) on your left. Shortly afterwards, turn right along an alleyway recently (and romantically) renamed Lovers Walk. At the end, cross Gallery Road and go through a gate into Belair Park, following link arrows and looking out for chiffchaff and dunnock, or pipistrelle, noctule and Daubenton's bats if dusk is approaching.

Cross a bridge over a stream and turn left along a sealed path. The water on your left is part of the ancient River Effra, most of which now flows underground. Pass a children's play area and, just before tennis courts, turn right and then left to exit the park. Cross the road at the lights and West Dulwich railway station is on your right, under the bridge.

Finsbury Park to Alexandra Palace

Distance 8km **Time** 3 hours
Start Manor House ⊖
Finish Alexandra Palace ⇌

Amble around Finsbury Park, then trace an abandoned railway line across north London from Stroud Green to Alexandra Palace, trundling behind the houses of Crouch End, Highgate and Muswell Hill, and passing ghost stations, bat-occupied tunnels and arches covered in stunning street art.

As you stroll, stay alert for the spriggan, a supernatural creature said to haunt this walk, which famously features in a story by modern-horror maestro Stephen King. But fear not, there's more light than shade on this escapade, which begins with a traverse of London's longest linear nature reserve, a verdant vehicleless corridor, rich in wildlife and popular with families, amblers, ramblers, birders, bike riders and runners.

Leave Manor House tube station via Exit 6 (Green Lanes North West Side). Turn right and walk through Finsbury Park's Manor Gate – open daily, dawn till dusk – into a green Victorian-era haven, created on the remnants of old Hornsey Wood to offer the poor population of north London some breathing and recreation space. Pass a lodge on your left, cross the inner ring road and follow a fingerpost pointing towards Oxford Road Gate. Keep bearing left at the next three forks in the path, passing broad oaks and colourful maple trees, and going through McKenzie Flower Garden. Turn right at the children's playground to reach the pond and walk with the water on your right. Here, squirrels scuttle between trees and the lake is lively with waterfowl, seemingly unfazed by fountains explosively erupting around them.

By the hire boats, bear left and walk towards the adventure playground, with Finsbury Park Café on your right. Turn right at the next path junction, joining the Capital Ring walking route. Use the zebra crossing on the inner circular road and continue straight ahead towards Oxford Road. Pass a fingerpost pointing to Highgate along the Capital Ring, cross a footbridge over train tracks and turn immediately right, setting off along the southern section of the Parkland Walk, tracing the route of the old Victorian railway line.

After being used for passenger and freight services from the 1860s to the 1960s, the rails were lifted in 1972 and the Parkland Walk opened in 1984. It quickly became popular and plans to turn the route into a road a few years later were robustly rejected. Declared a Local Nature Reserve in 1990, the track has also become a crucial car-free corridor for endangered urban amblers such as hedgehogs.

Walk along the broad unsealed path, passing a numbered wooden post indicating the nearby presence of a miniature painting done on chewing gum (honestly), by artist Ben Wilson, part of a series of such works along the route. Continue over a bridge, crossing Upper Tollington Park road, and stroll along the raised track which chugs along between houses and enters a tunnel of overhanging branches. Some 50 bird species flitter and twitter amid the ash, birch, holm oak, holly, hawthorn, rowan, yew, sycamore, apple and cherry trees that have flourished since the trains stopped. Look out for finches, goldcrests, redpolls, long-tailed tits, jays, woodpeckers, nuthatches and even the occasional hovering kestrel.

Cross a couple of bridges overlooking Stroud Green, their concrete flanks colourful with graffiti. A footpath soon branches right to clamber along the side of the cutting, but the main track rolls under a bridge, where an information board describes the butterflies that enjoy this acid grassland habitat. Continue under

two more bridges, resplendent with urban artwork, and pass an adventure playground on your left.

A fingerpost points off-route towards Crouch Hill, but keep rolling straight towards Highgate. Ignore a path rising to the left, and go under a footbridge to reach long-abandoned Crouch End station, where full-length platforms remain in place on either side of the track, and a pictorial information board transports you back in time to the railway's heyday. In one of the arches, you might spot the fantastical figure of a spriggan emerging from the brickwork. Created by artist Marilyn Collins, this sculpture portrays a ghostly goatman said to haunt the path – an urban myth that apparently inspired American author Stephen King to write a short story called *Crouch End*, after he stayed with a friend nearby and walked this trail.

Steps to the side lead to a good café at road level here, if you're in need of sustenance. Otherwise, continue under the bridge along the gently rising track, through another tunnel of trees. Cross bridges over Stanhope Road and Northwood Road and pass a garden on your right, by a couple of old-fashioned streetlamps, where Friends of the Parkland Walk have created a small woodland trail, complete with insect lodges, bug hotels, hedgehog houses, bat boxes, bird feeders and a frog pond.

The old railway track disappears into the dusk of a long-ago sealed tunnel

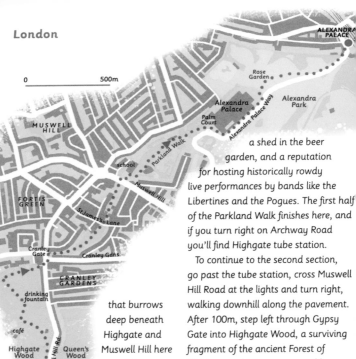

a shed in the beer garden, and a reputation for hosting historically rowdy live performances by bands like the Libertines and the Pogues. The first half of the Parkland Walk finishes here, and if you turn right on Archway Road you'll find Highgate tube station.

To continue to the second section, go past the tube station, cross Muswell Hill Road at the lights and turn right, walking downhill along the pavement. After 100m, step left through Gypsy Gate into Highgate Wood, a surviving fragment of the ancient Forest of Middlesex, which once covered huge swathes of London and surrounding counties. Walk along a path running parallel to Muswell Hill Road, ignoring the first right turn (for New Gate). At the next junction, bear left and follow signage towards the café, wandering through oak, hornbeam, holly and wild service, and listening for woodpeckers. Where the Pavilion Café

that burrows deep beneath Highgate and Muswell Hill here – providing a home for bats – so you have to hit the streets. Bear left, ascend to Holmesdale Road, then turn right and walk uphill to meet Archway Road and The Boogaloo, a legendary pub with London's best jukebox, a radio station operating from

s arrowed left, go right through enchanting woodland to an obelisk-esque drinking fountain. Bear left here and follow the Capital Ring route to the T-junction by Bridge Gate, where you turn right along the path to exit the woods via Cranley Gate.

Cross Muswell Hill Road at the lights, turning left and then right, very briefly, into Cranley Gardens (one-time address of serial killer Dennis Nilsen, who lived at No 23). By the road sign at the very top of the road is the entrance to the northern section of the Parkland Walk. Descend steps here, turn right and follow the old railway line across a bridge and along an elevated section with a big drop-off to the right, offering excellent views over London. Continue past Hillfield Park Gate, over St James's Lane and through an underpass beneath Muswell Hill. Go right, then left, following signage for Alexandra Park and Palace.

Stroll along a raised walkway into Alexandra Park and bear left, passing the Grove Café. When the path forks keep left, following an Alexandra Palace pointer. At the next junction, continue straight, ascending to the grand Palm Court entrance to Alexandra Palace. Turn right and loop around the impressive building – a bastion of British broadcasting used by the BBC for decades – enjoying more amazing views across London and into neighbouring counties.

Pass the antennae-topped BBC Tower, go through the car park opposite the ice-skating rink entrance and descend through the Rose Garden. At a T-junction, turn right and then bear left along a path descending the hill. At the bottom, carefully cross and veer left along Bedford Road. After 80m, look out for a small walkway leading right, over a footbridge, into Alexandra Palace station.

Bushy Park and Hampton Court

Distance 10km **Time** 3 hours 30
Start Hampton Wick ⇌
Finish Hampton Wick or Kingston ⇌

This half-day hike dawdles across a once royal hunting ground — now more famous as the birthplace of the international phenomenon that is parkrun — before dropping you back in time at the gates of historic Hampton Court, Henry VIII's favourite hang out. You can bail here, roughly halfway around, by heading across the river and hopping on a train at Hampton Court station, but then you'd miss looping back via lovely leafy Barge Walk, which runs along the riverbank to Kingston-upon-Thames.

Leave Hampton Wick station by the exit/entrance with the ticket office (next to Platform 2). Cross High Street at the lights and turn left. Head right on School Road, and then go left along Park Road by the Assembly Rooms House. Opposite the Foresters Arms, go right along St John's Road and walk to the church of the same name at the end of the street. Cross Church Grove at the zebra crossing and go through a heavy metal gate into Bushy Park, passing a London Loop waymarker on the wall.

Walk past tennis courts, a skate park and sports grounds on your left, and continue along an avenue between parallel fences, lined with conker-laden horse chestnut trees. Go through another metal gate and walk straight ahead with a cricket ground on your right. Leave the gravel track and hug the edge of the cricket pitch. After crossing a second wide track, take a path leading diagonally right across the grass, passing to the right of a copse of trees 200m away. Follow London Loop waymarkers (not always easy to see), looking out for hovering skylarks as you keep the trees on your left. This is a great area for spotting some of the park's population of fallow deer (present since Tudor times, when Henry VIII hunted them) and larger red deer, which are indigenous to Britain but were brought

145

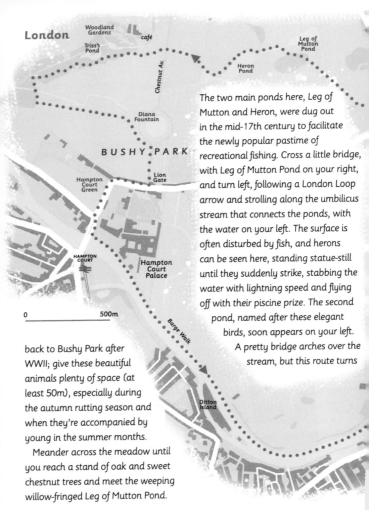

The two main ponds here, Leg of Mutton and Heron, were dug out in the mid-17th century to facilitate the newly popular pastime of recreational fishing. Cross a little bridge, with Leg of Mutton Pond on your right, and turn left, following a London Loop arrow and strolling along the umbilicus stream that connects the ponds, with the water on your left. The surface is often disturbed by fish, and herons can be seen here, standing statue-still until they suddenly strike, stabbing the water with lightning speed and flying off with their piscine prize. The second pond, named after these elegant birds, soon appears on your left. A pretty bridge arches over the stream, but this route turns

back to Bushy Park after WWII; give these beautiful animals plenty of space (at least 50m), especially during the autumn rutting season and when they're accompanied by young in the summer months.

Meander across the meadow until you reach a stand of oak and sweet chestnut trees and meet the weeping willow-fringed Leg of Mutton Pond.

146

right to ramble around Heron Pond, walking with the rippling water to the left. Ignore tracks going right and keep tracing the bank, crossing a couple of small bridges and following London Loop waymarkers on wooden posts as they lead you around this fish-shaped pond, with the tail formed by the long-abandoned Boating Pool. At the top of this tail, ignore the bridge leading left to the car park and go straight ahead, keeping the feeder stream on your left (a London Loop arrow points the way, but it's easy to miss).

At the head of the feeder stream, bear left, go past a large water pump and cross the tarmac of Chestnut Avenue.

Follow London Loop waymarkers across the grass on the other side, walking through a plantation of beech trees until you meet a gravel path next to another stream. Keep the water on your right and trace the stream and the London Loop route to enter the Woodland Gardens, a tranquil expanse of trees and shrubs that explodes into colour in spring and provides a playground for scampering squirrels and multiple woodland birds. (If you're exploring with a dog you'll need to stay out of the gardens, but just walk around the woodland, keeping the fence on your right until you rejoin the main route at the sealed path by the bridge.) The pleasant Pheasantry Café is off to the right if you fancy refreshments, but otherwise continue through the mixed-species woods, past Triss's Pond, until you exit the first section of the gardens. Go straight ahead and then, just before the gate into the next section of the gardens, leave the London Loop and turn left, following a sealed path over a bridge across a stream.

Keep going along this path until you cross a broad grassy boulevard lined with trees. Turn left here and stroll towards the Diana Fountain in the near distance (a sealed path runs parallel to this greenway, which is useful in wet weather).

The fantastic fountain forms the centrepiece of Christopher Wren's Chestnut Avenue. Dedicated to the Roman goddess of knowledge and hunting, it's crowned by a golden statue of Arethusa, a water nymph transformed into a fountain by Diana. Turn right at the fountain and follow Chestnut Avenue to the Lion Gate, where you exit the park opposite Hampton Court. Use the zebra crossing to go over the road to the gates of Henry VIII's beloved palace, which remained a royal residence on the edge of the capital for two centuries after his rule, with a gap in the middle when the monarchy was dissolved and Oliver Cromwell used the place as his weekend house. Turn right and walk past the Kings Arms Hotel, following Hampton Court Road as it arcs left around the palace. Stay left at the roundabout and then turn left to reach the riverside just before Hampton Court Bridge, opposite the Mute Swan pub.

Stroll along a scenic section of the Thames Path known as Barge Walk, with the extravagantly ornate gardens and buildings of Hampton Court on your left, where kings, queens and courtiers once cavorted amid flowing fountains and florid flowerbeds. The shared path soon splits, sending cyclists slightly left; stay right and walk along the smaller unsealed footpath that hugs the riverside, where willow, sycamore, ash, hawthorn and the occasional crab apple tree cling to the bank. Hike past houseboats, as mute swans, moorhens, coots, ducks and paddleboarders pootle along the majestic waterway, and optimistic anglers dangle their lines from various vantage points.

Just after tree-covered Ditton Island, the bank bends left and you pass a chunky wooden bench. On the other side of the cycle track here is Ditton Gate, which leads into Home Park, a publicly accessible part of the old palace grounds that you can explore if you fancy searching for more deer among the greens of Hampton Court Palace Golf Club. However, this route continues along beautiful Barge Walk, passing the suburbia of Surbiton and Seething Wells on the opposite bank. Eventually the bike track rejoins the footpath, which becomes a broad gravel track, lined with juicy blackberries and flowering purple loosestrife in summer. This takes you past Ravens Ait, an island in the river used for private parties, and Surbiton Passage Gate (another entry point into Home Park).

Once the path becomes sealed, the impressive buildings of Kingston-upon-Thames start to dominate the view on the far bank, with the roofs of the university, square-topped church, college and courthouse sculpting the skyline. Walk beneath the boughs of big conker trees towards the five lovely arches of Kingston Bridge, as the path passes a few enviably positioned residential homes on the left and huddles of houseboats in Richmond moorings. On the other side of the Thames, restaurants begin to line the riverbank.

Follow Barge Walk as it leans left and ascends to meet Kingston Bridge. From here, you have a choice: either turn right and walk along the wonderfully named Horse Fair to cross the river and head towards Kingston station, or go left and then right to hike along High Street back to Hampton Wick station.

Hackney Marshes and Walthamstow Wetlands

Distance 11km **Time** 4 hours
Start Bromley-by-Bow ⊖
Finish Tottenham Hale ⊖ ≋

**Created by an Act of Parliament
as a 'green lung' for London
(and Essex and Hertfordshire),
Lee Valley Regional Park is a
lush expanse of river-fed
wilderness right next to the
East End. Stretching across
4000 hectares, its delightful
waterways, wetlands, marshes
and meadows are populated
by a wealth of wildlife and
enjoyed by hikers, bikers,
birders and boaters.**

This route rambles from Bromley to
Tottenham, tracing the Lee (often
written 'Lea') past magnificent (or
monstrous, depending on your view)
modern structures created for the 2012
London Olympics, before hiking
through Hackney and Walthamstow
Marshes to an expansive wetlands.

Leave Bromley-by-Bow tube station
and go left, down some steps, before
turning right through an underpass,
following fingerposts for Limehouse Cut
Canal. Emerge, walk straight through
Leaside Lock, bear left opposite
Riverstone Heights and head along
little Imperial Street. Turn right at the
end, pass the supermarket and go right
again along Three Mill Lane. Cross a
bridge over the River Lee, walking onto
Three Mills Island, passing a Lee Valley
information board and ambling along
an attractive cobbled lane, past the
Clock Mill on your right.

Bear left and walk with the
waterway on your left and Three Mills
Green on the right, passing a sculpture
of joined hands, a memorial to several
people who drowned here in 1901.
Keep going straight, with the park on
your right, until a bridge takes you off
Three Mills Island. Follow a fingerpost
for Three Mills Wall River and Dane's
Yard, walking along a footpath with
Waterworks River on your left and
residential houses on the right. Pass a
large sculpture of the Olympic torch
(which resembles a giant spiral of

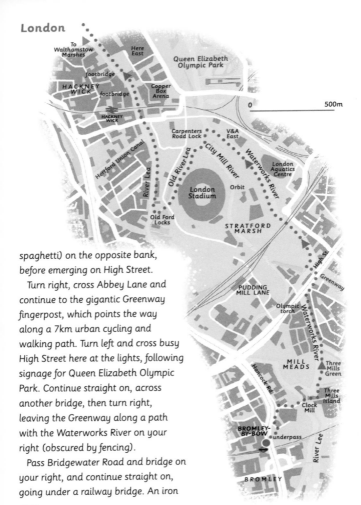

To Walthamstow Marshes

Here East

Queen Elizabeth Olympic Park

footbridge

HACKNEY WICK

footbridge

Copper Box Arena

0   500m

HACKNEY WICK

Carpenters Road Lock

V&A East

London Aquatics Centre

Hertford Union Canal

River Lea

Old River Lea

City Mill River

Waterworks River

London Stadium

Orbit

Old Ford Locks

STRATFORD MARSH

High St

Greenway

PUDDING MILL LANE

Olympic torch

Waterworks River

MILL MEADS

Three Mills Green

Hancock Rd

Three Mills Island

Clock Mill

BROMLEY-BY-BOW

underpass

River Lee

BROMLEY

spaghetti) on the opposite bank, before emerging on High Street.

Turn right, cross Abbey Lane and continue to the gigantic Greenway fingerpost, which points the way along a 7km urban cycling and walking path. Turn left and cross busy High Street here at the lights, following signage for Queen Elizabeth Olympic Park. Continue straight on, across another bridge, then turn right, leaving the Greenway along a path with the Waterworks River on your right (obscured by fencing).

Pass Bridgewater Road and bridge on your right, and continue straight on, going under a railway bridge. An iron bridge crosses the river on the right, while on your left is the ever-expanding East Bank, a new cultural quarter with performance spaces, recording studios and education centres.

Dominating the skyline here is the extraordinary *Orbit*, a chaotic-looking 114.5m-high structure designed by Turner Prize-winning artist Anish Kapoor and engineer-artist Cecil Balmond, which is simultaneously Britain's biggest public artwork, an observation tower and – since 2016 – a titanic tunnel slide. Before the 2012 Olympics, the *Orbit* was heralded by then-London mayor Boris Johnson as a legacy project of the Games that would become the UK capital's equivalent of the Eiffel Tower. Unfortunately, reactions to its unveiling ranged from complete confusion to furious negativity and the structure has underperformed spectacularly as a visitor attraction ever since, despite the rather desperate addition of the slide.

Keep walking along the waterside, with the Aquatics Centre and new V&A building on the opposite bank. To your left, across City Mill River, is the London Stadium, now home to West Ham United football club. Pass under a couple of bridges and trace the path around a left bend to Carpenter's Road Lock. Here, cross a metal bridge covered in tram tracks, following a fingerpost for Hackney Wick, Fish Island and Old Ford Locks.

Go straight ahead, under a large bridge, with the London Stadium on your left and the River Lee on the right. Pass beneath more bridges and, after ducking under big pipes, cross the footbridge leading right to Old Ford Locks. Ignore the next footbridge and instead stroll straight ahead, past lock gates, walking with the River Lea Navigaton on your left. Keep following Lea Valley Walk and Capital Ring waymarkers, and signage for Hackney Wick, to ramble past riverboats and go under another bridge. Just after the Hertford Union Canal joins the River Lea Navigation from the left, you pass Barge East, a boat-based restaurant and bar, and go under a roadbridge. If you've had enough, head across this bridge and follow White Post Lane to Hackney Wick train station. Otherwise, continue along the towpath, going under a railway bridge (enlivened with excellent graffiti art) and then a footbridge.

The bank is busy with houseboats of all shapes and sizes here, with people leading largely off-grid lifestyles, while community and creative spaces proliferate on the other side of the navigation. Go past East Wick moorings, walk under another pedestrian bridge, then pass Here East, a modern development with offices and bars occupying the former Olympic Media Centre. Keep walking along the towpath, following fingerposts for Hackney Marshes and passing under two large roadbridges. Happily, the traffic cacophony is rapidly replaced by the rustling of leaves from native trees in Wick Woodland, on your right.

Pass under Marshgate Bridge, encouraged on by enthusiastic shouts emanating from the football fields that cover Hackney Marshes, off to the right beyond the trees. Keep going, beneath a footbridge backed by a glass-and-mirror statue half-hidden in the foliage. Continue under Cow Bridge, then duck into the Middlesex Filter Beds Nature Reserve on your right, where bird hides offer an opportunity to spy species including snipe, sandpiper, teal, godwit, pochard, little grebe and gadwall, plus toads, frogs, newts and dragonflies. You'll also find *Nature's Throne* and *Hackney Henge* in here, sculptures created from Cornish granite by Bromley-based artist Paula Haughney.

Rejoin the path, which soon crosses the water to Millfields Park, before passing the point where the River Lea Navigation and the River Lee become

one, opposite the Princess of Wales.
Go past the pub and under Lea Bridge
(which leads right to Lea Bridge train
station if you're ready to bail). If not,
continue along the Capital Ring route,
with the river on your right and North
Millfields Park on the left. Pass some
flats and then cross back to the other
bank by turning right over King's Head
footbridge. Stroll along a broad gravel
track with the river on your left and
Lee Valley Park on the right, before
crossing a cattle grid and entering

155

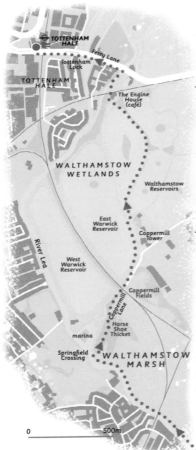

Walthamstow Marshes Nature Reserve. Go under a railway bridge covered in stunning street art and featuring a blue plaque celebrating A V Roe, who made the first all-British powered flight from here in 1909.

Keep tracing the bank until you see Horseshoe Bridge spanning the river at Springfield Crossing. Turn right here, crossing a sealed track and following a footpath through Horse Shoe Thicket. Bear left at the fork, emerge next to Lee Valley Marina Springfield gates, turn right again and follow signage for Walthamstow Wetlands along Coppermill Lane, passing Coppermill Fields on your right. Duck beneath a low railway bridge and, 100m later, hook left into Walthamstow Wetlands, a fantastic free-to-visit wildlife haven that's open daily until an hour before dusk. (If it's shut, return to Springfield Crossing, go over the footbridge, turn right and walk along the River Lee to Ferry Lane.)

Once in the wetlands, walk

with Coppermill Stream on your right and East Warwick Reservoir on the left, passing the Coppermill Tower, a watermill constructed in 1806 with an Italianate top added later. About 100m beyond the tower, turn acute right and cross the stream, before bearing left to walk past a pylon and stroll along a track that wends and bends between Reservoirs 1 and 2 and 3, passing blooming gorse, stealthy twitchers and somnambulant anglers amid inconsolable weeping willows and happy picnickers perched on pontoons.

The tracks converge at the Engine House where there is a café, toilets, an elevated viewing platform and an excellent information centre. Built in 1894 to house a triple expansion engine and later extended to accommodate steam turbines, it now features a new chimney (with added nesting boxes for swifts) replacing the original which was demolished in the 1960s.

Exit the wetlands, turn left along Ferry Lane, cross the bridge over the River Lee by Tottenham Lock, and continue to Tottenham Hale station.

Oxleas Wood to the Thames Barrier

Distance 10km **Time** 4 hours
Start Falconwood ⮂
Finish Charlton ⮂

Climb through the 8000-year-old forest of Oxleas Wood to the folly of Severndroog Castle on the broad shoulders of Shooter's Hill – where archers once practised and executed highwaymen were hung in gibbets – before wandering through historic Woolwich and Charlton to the Thames Barrier, which protects London from drowning.

From Falconwood station, turn right along Lingfield Crescent. Cross Rochester Way at the traffic island, turn right and stroll over the railway bridge, following a Green Chain Walk (GCW) arrow on a lamppost for Eltham Park North. By a bus stop, turn left into Shepherdleas Wood. When the path splits, bear right, cross a small bridge over a creek and trace yellow arrows through sweet chestnut trees. At the next junction, turn right and amble through beech, holly,

hawthorn and towering oaks. Meeting an Eltham Park North fingerpost, go straight ahead, picking up GCW arrows pointing towards 'Oxleas Wood and Thames Barrier'.

Keep following yellow arrows to re-emerge on Rochester Way. Cross at the lights and briefly walk along Welling Way before turning left into Oxleas Wood. Plans to build a new road and bridge across the Thames that would have decimated this deciduous forest were defeated in the 1990s by local protests. Safe for the foreseeable future, this forest on the flanks of Shooter's Hill is a sensational place to explore in any season, but during spring the woods are awash with bluebells.

Turn right when you meet a wide track and follow GCW waymarkers through oak, holly, hawthorn, sweet chestnut, beech, silver birch, hornbeam, hazel and rare wild service trees. At the edge of Oxleas Meadow, turn right to wander along a wide green avenue to a fingerpost, then turn left, following the arm pointing towards 'Woolwich

159

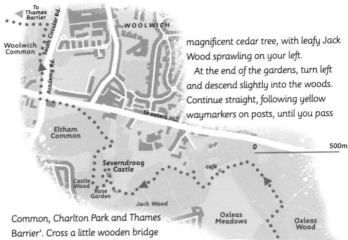

magnificent cedar tree, with leafy Jack Wood sprawling on your left.

At the end of the gardens, turn left and descend slightly into the woods. Continue straight, following yellow waymarkers on posts, until you pass

Common, Charlton Park and Thames Barrier'. Cross a little wooden bridge and take the smaller path leading uphill, tracing GCW waymarkers. Turn left at the next junction, ascend some more and then go straight ahead to emerge by the Oxleas Wood Café.

Go straight ahead at the next fingerpost, down a sealed path into trees. At the bottom of the dip, at a fork, go slightly right and follow the path as it arcs right and climbs to a GCW fingerpost at a T-junction. Turn left and walk along a wider sealed track through a manicured grassy garden area, with the ornate red brick walls of the Memorial Hospital on your right. Continue past a

a pretty cottage (the old lodge of long-gone Castle Wood House) on your left. Here, branch right and walk uphill along a gently curving sealed lane. At the top, turn sharp left to arrive at the feet of towering Severndroog Castle, a Gothic-style folly complete with castellated turrets, built in 1784 as a memorial to Sir William James, director of the East India Company. The mock castle offers fabulous 360-degree views of London and seven counties from its lofty viewing platform (open most Sundays), plus galleries and a tearoom.

Stroll around the castle, then follow GCW and Capital Ring arrows down the hill, passing beneath the boughs of a big oak. Descend steps towards the rose garden, positioned where Castle Wood House once stood, enjoying panoramic views across Eltham. Note the twisted trunk of a sweet chestnut tree on your left, before continuing down the steps and following the path right to exit the rose garden, passing a massive sequoia tree on the left as you leave.

While walking along a sealed track through Castle Wood, look and listen out for rare wood warblers, nuthatch and woodpeckers. When the path forks, keep right, staying on the high ground and walking along a sealed track through

a tunnel of oak, sweet chestnut, holly and sycamore.

At a fingerpost, turn left along the GCW, following a pointer for 'Woolwich Common via Eltham Common', before bearing left and descending shallow steps through swaying sycamore trees.

Emerge on Eltham Common by Shooters Hill Road, a thoroughfare where highwaymen once terrorised travellers. Trace the pointers across the green, walking parallel to the road before joining the pavement by a road sign pointing right for the Woolwich Ferry. Follow the fingerpost for Woolwich Common and Charlton Park, turning right to cross Shooters Hill Road at the lights and then going straight along Academy Road. After 200m, turn left along a footpath, following a GCW fingerpost for Charlton Park and the Thames Barrier.

Keep following waymarkers, heading straight and then left along

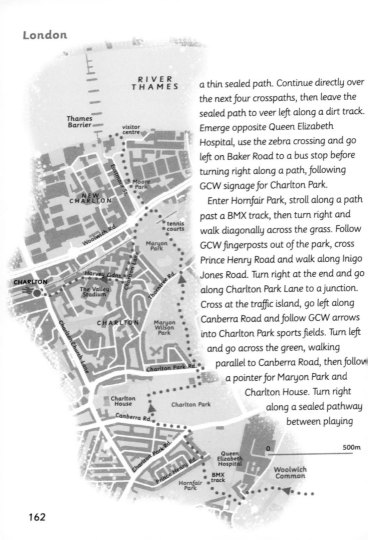

a thin sealed path. Continue directly over the next four crosspaths, then leave the sealed path to veer left along a dirt track. Emerge opposite Queen Elizabeth Hospital, use the zebra crossing and go left on Baker Road to a bus stop before turning right along a path, following GCW signage for Charlton Park.

Enter Hornfair Park, stroll along a path past a BMX track, then turn right and walk diagonally across the grass. Follow GCW fingerposts out of the park, cross Prince Henry Road and walk along Inigo Jones Road. Turn right at the end and go along Charlton Park Lane to a junction. Cross at the traffic island, go left along Canberra Road and follow GCW arrows into Charlton Park sports fields. Turn left and go across the green, walking parallel to Canberra Road, then follow a pointer for Maryon Park and Charlton House. Turn right along a sealed pathway between playing

162

fields, with Charlton House – a 17th-century Jacobean mansion – off to your left. Go right again along another sealed path, with a skatepark on your left, pass a children's play area and turn left, following an arrow for Maryon Wilson Park and the Thames Barrier.

Leave Charlton Park, turn right, use the zebra crossing, then hook left into Maryon Wilson Park. Stroll through this leafy public park and nature reserve, originally part of the ancient Hanging Wood that covered much of Woolwich and Charlton and was notoriously haunted by highwaymen, before being enclosed within the Charlton Manor Estate, occupied by the Maryon Wilson family between 1767 and 1925. When the path forks at a stream, go right and then straight, keeping the stream on your left. Pass an animal enclosure, with sheep, goats, fallow deer and more, and follow a Thames Barrier pointer.

Go straight over the next junction and up the hill. Cross Thorntree Road and wander through the green opposite into Maryon Park (formerly a sandpit within the Maryon Wilson Estate). Go through a gate and down steps before turning right

and going down more stairs. Bear left at the bottom, passing tennis courts on your right and then turning left along a sealed path, past a children's play area. Exit the park on busy Woolwich Road.

Cross at the lights, bear left and then turn right along a footpath running parallel to Eastmoor Street, meandering through Moore Park to the waterside, where the futuristic hulks of the Thames Barrier span the river, ready to protect central London from cataclysmic flooding. These barriers, on the sea side of the capital, are shut if rising water levels pose a danger, preventing nightmarish scenarios such as the Thames breaking its banks and water filling the London Underground. Well worth exploring, the Thames Barrier Information Centre is away to your right.

Return to Maryon Park, turn right and walk through the lower section along a path running parallel to Woolwich Road, before turning left along Charlton Lane. Head right along Harvey Gardens, passing The Valley, Charlton Athletic FC's stadium, and following Floyd Road to Charlton Church Lane. Charlton station is just to the right.

26

Epping Forest

Distance 6.5km (8km including
Pole Hill) **Time** 2–3 hours
Start & Finish Chingford ⇌

**Explore London's largest forest,
trekking past a Tudor hunting
lodge and venturing into the
heart of an historic wilderness
saved from enclosure in the 1800s
by the capital's common people
who – in Europe's first ever
environmentally-focused
campaign of direct action –
successfully defended our right
to roam these enchanting woods.**

Whisper thanks to those pioneers of
access activism as you escape the urban
jungle and step into the woody embrace
of epic Epping Forest, which stretches
beyond Greater London, deep into Essex.
Amid the canopy of oak, beech, silver
birch, hornbeam, hawthorn and holly,
around 55,000 ancient 'veteran' trees
stand in these woodlands, some of
which were alive prior to the Norman
invasion in 1066. This hike has many
highlights, including eye-popping views
from the peak of Pole Hill if you do the

optional extra loop, but you could spend
every weekend of the year here, delving
deeper and discovering new treasures.

Leave Chingford station and turn right
along Station Road. After Beresford
Road, use the traffic island to transfer to
the other side of the main road, which
soon segues into Ranger's Road. Cross
Bury Road, pass Epping Forest signage
and continue ascending the gradual tree-
fringed hill for 250m, until you reach the
Royal Forest hotel. Beside this inn is an
Epping Forest Visitor Centre and the
Queen Elizabeth Hunting Lodge, which
Henry VIII had built in 1543 so he could
observe deer on Chingford Chase. No red
or roe deer remain in Epping Forest, but
you might spot fallow deer or, if you're
very lucky, little muntjacs (originally a
southeast Asian species). Open Tuesday
to Sunday, 10am–4pm (longer during
summer), the visitor centre is a font of
free information about the forest and its
wildlife, and has toilet facilities.

Walk between the visitor centre and
the historic hunting lodge, passing
through a gate guarded by two wooden
deer, and turn right, following an arrow

for the Willow Trail and glancing across the great green immensity of Epping Forest to your left. Look out for free-roaming Longhorn cattle – these large cows with colossal curled horns graze here in summer, a process that promotes the growth of plants like pepper saxifrage and bird's foot trefoil, which in turn attract butterflies and bees.

Pass an obelisk, a water fountain and several picnic tables connected to Butler's Retreat café, housed in a restored Essex barn on your right – a good place to grab a coffee and cake, or something more substantial, before continuing to a fingerpost and following the arm pointing towards Connaught Water.

Descend the wide track, ignoring paths branching left and right. At the bottom of the hill, when you meet a level gravelly area, follow the red Willow Trail arrow pointing acute right. Take the next left, following another arrow, and trace a well-formed track leading to Connaught Water, an attractive artificial lake enjoyed by walkers, runners, families and fishers, which was originally created in the 19th century and now hosts an abundance of waterfowl, from coots, moorhens, swans, geese and goosanders to flamboyant mandarin ducks and great crested grebes. Around its banks, stealthy heron hunt in the shallows and anglers and photographers seek quietude, while children run amok along boardwalks.

At the lake's edge, turn right and follow a fingerpost for Connaught Water car park. Continue walking with the water on your left, going along the boardwalk. At the end of the wooden walkway go right, and then left at the fingerpost, following the arm pointing towards High Beach along the Willow Trail. Wander along a wide well-formed track with Connaught Brook babbling to your right. Eventually the brook flows underneath the path, and shortly afterwards a red arrow points left. Follow this over a bridge across the stream and bear left, heeding another arrow directing you up a gently ascending track.

When you meet an obvious junction, pause and contemplate the mighty oak

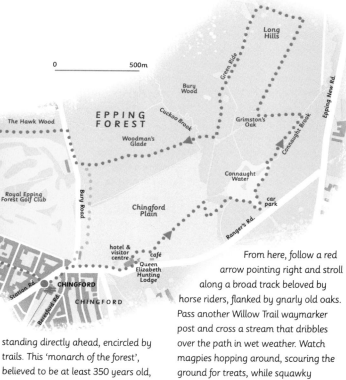

standing directly ahead, encircled by trails. This 'monarch of the forest', believed to be at least 350 years old, is named Grimston's Oak after a local cricketing hero, but it's also often called Bedford's Oak in honour of John T Bedford, who played a leading role in the fight to save the forest in the 1870s.

From here, follow a red arrow pointing right and stroll along a broad track beloved by horse riders, flanked by gnarly old oaks. Pass another Willow Trail waymarker post and cross a stream that dribbles over the path in wet weather. Watch magpies hopping around, scouring the ground for treats, while squawky parakeets prance in the branches – these exotic visitors, now common in parks across the capital, made Epping Forest their early London base, with a breeding pair observed here in the 1930s. More melodic birdsong comes courtesy of traditional woodland species – including warblers, cuckoo, chats and thrushes – although their solos are often interrupted by the machine-gun rat-a-tat of great spotted woodpeckers.

From the next major junction, turn left, following a red arrow up the gentle rise of Long Hills. Bear left at a Y-junction and trace the arcing track past two waymarker posts (one with a yellow arrow, the other a red) – both are pointing in the right direction. The wide track ascends slowly to a crest with a small pond beside the trail. From here, follow another pair of yellow and red waymarkers to a cross-tracks. Ignore the red arrow pointing straight ahead (and disregard the yellow and red arrows visible further on) and instead turn right here to cross Cuckoo Brook and stroll along a particularly pleasant path. Just before Bury Road, a wide track intersects your path and you have a choice to make.

To head directly back to the station, turn left along the track, walk out of the woods and across the open meadow of Chingford Plain, then continue parallel to the road until you meet a wooden post with a London Loop waymarker pointing right, and follow this through Bury Road car park and past the golf course (on the right) to reach Ranger's/Station Road, which leads right into Chingford.

Alternatively, for the Pole Hill extension, turn right along the track that runs parallel to Bury Road. Pass a London Loop waymarker on a wooden post and continue for 150m until a second London Loop arrow directs you left. Carefully cross the road here and pick up the footpath directly opposite, entering the Hawk Wood. The trail braids a bit as you stroll through the trees, but all threads lead in the same direction (the path on the left, near the golf course, is generally drier). Through gaps in the branches on your right, sunlight can sometimes be seen glistening off King George's Reservoir, way below. When the London Loop arcs right, towards Yardley Hill, this route turns left, up Pole Hill (the London Loop waymarker is on the lower path, but the upper path naturally leads left, so just follow it round).

The path becomes tangled again, but just avoid the golf course and keep descending until you reach a clearing with spectacular views across London, and an obelisk. Built in 1824 by the Astronomer Royal, the Reverend John Pond, this pointy landmark lay directly on the Greenwich Meridian line (as it was then), due north of Greenwich, and was used by Royal Observatory geographers to set telescopes and other astronomical equipment. In 1850 (34 years before being adopted as the planet's Prime Meridian) the line was tweaked, and it now runs 5.8m east of the obelisk, where an Ordnance Survey trig point stands.

Besides the obelisk and a stunning view, Pole Hill's major claim to fame is that after WWI, the officer, diplomat, archaeologist and writer T E Lawrence (better known as 'Lawrence of Arabia', thanks to the epic David Lean film of the same name made about his life and based on the autobiographical book *Seven Pillars of Wisdom*) built a hut – complete with a plunge pool – on the western side of the hill, overlooking the reservoirs. Lawrence originally planned to set up a boutique printing press and live here.

You need to descend the opposite side, however. Looking at the obelisk from the direction you arrived, turn left by the bench and descend the path. Just before reaching Mornington Road, turn left along a dirt track, walking with houses on your right. Turn right through the next cut-through and follow Connaught Avenue to the station.

27

The River Wandle from Colliers Wood to the Thames

Distance 10km **Time** 3 hours 30
Start Colliers Wood ⊖
Finish Putney Bridge ⊖

Follow the flow of the wistful River Wandle, a rare chalk stream, as it snakes through south London to join the Thames in Wandsworth. While the surrounds oscillate between pretty and gritty, this tale-drenched urban waterway historically powered plenty of local industries, and now the river supports a wealth of wildlife.

Exit Portland stone-clad Colliers Wood tube station, turn briefly left and cross High Street at the traffic lights. Walk directly ahead along Baltic Close and past The Holden pub, named after the architect, Charles Holden, who designed Colliers Wood station and many other London Transport buildings. Go between two brick posts bearing the words 'Wandle Valley' and enter Merton's Wandle Park.

Not to be confused with a park of the same name further upstream in Croydon, this 4.5-hectare green space covers ground once occupied by Wandle Bank House, built in 1791 by James Perry, a mill owner and editor of the popular and occasionally radical newspaper *The Morning Chronicle*.

Go straight ahead along a sealed path and across two bridges spanning the remains of waterways that once powered Perry's Merton Mill. After the second bridge, bear right and pass a memorial fountain to Harry Pollard Ashby and Robert Broomfield Fenwick, later occupants of Wandle Bank and benefactors of nearby All Saints' Church, who advocated for more open areas for locals.

Go straight, then left across a bridge over the Wandle. Turn right and walk along the road, parallel to the river, which soon flows under Connolly's Mill building. There's been a mill here for more than seven centuries, but the current brick building (converted into flats in 1994) was designed by Scottish engineering genius John Rennie

London

To Wandsworth

EARLSFIELD

Penwith Road

Garfield Lane

Summerley St.

weirs

EARLSFIELD

Steerforth St.

Garratt Park

SUMMERSTOWN

Wandle Trail

Plough Lane Stadium

Plough Lane

River Wandle

Lambeth Cemetery

HAYDONS ROAD

Wandle Meadow Nature Park

SOUTH WIMBLEDON

North Rd.

COLLIERS WOOD

Byegrove Rd.

Connolly's Mill

Wandle Park

COLLIERS WOOD

0   500m

in 1789. Once London's largest flour supplier, Merton Mill was later bought by Connolly's Ltd and turned into a leatherworks, supplying seating material for high-end car brands like Bentley and Rolls-Royce, and the benches in the Houses of Parliament.

Go straight across Byegrove Road and walk along a gravel path hugging the riverbank, with the water rushing on your right. Cross a bridge and follow the path as it ducks under a low bridge and strays away from the water briefly into Wandle Meadow Nature Park. A sewage works until 1970, this semi-wetlands was subsequently saved from hosting Wimbledon FC's stadium and is now a Local Nature Reserve, home to frogs, toads, newts and dragonflies, plus breeding populations of bullfinches, whitethroats and reed buntings.

Pass to the left of a pylon, trace the gravel path as it arcs across the park and when you meet a sealed track, go right. Turn left at a fingerpost, following pointers for Plough

172

The River Wandle from Colliers Wood to the Thames

Lane and Summerstown, and go under a railway bridge. Pass a Wandle Trail waymarker and stroll along the sealed path, with concrete sidings and the railway line off to your left, passing through cherry plum trees that produce blizzards of blossom each spring. A metal viewing platform on the left overlooks the confluence of the Wandle and the River Graveney, which flows in from the east (mostly underground) from Norbury. This was once the base of the Surrey Iron Railway, one of the world's first public railways when it opened in 1803, using horse-drawn carriages to transport coal, lime and manure between Wandsworth and Croydon.

Return to the main trail and keep walking with the water on your left, passing Wandle Trail signage to meet Plough Lane, home to Wimbledon FC's stadium (off to the right). Cross at the lights, turn left, then immediately right and walk along a sealed path, shared by hikers and bikers, with the river on your right. Grey wagtails hide among huddles of hazel trees along this lovely woody section of the trail. Pass a fingerpost for Earlsfield and look across the water to allotments and Garratt Park. Hunting heron stalk the shallows while coots and tufted ducks float past, cormorants dive and kingfishers plunge for prey.

When you meet another sealed path, turn right. The river splits briefly here to tumble down a pair of weirs. Turn right and cross the bridge overlooking the cascades. At the junction with Steerforth Street, turn left along Summerley Street. When you meet busy Garratt Lane, turn left, pass Earlsfield station, go under the railway bridge and walk through the vibrant suburb. Pass The Wandle pub and continue until you meet a Wandle Trail fingerpost pointing left along St John's Drive towards Riverside Walk and King George's Park. Stroll through flats, passing under three arches to emerge in a leafy area. Bear right, then left, crossing a footbridge over the Wandle and entering King George's Park, a large green place that's been providing outdoor recreation opportunities for locals for over a century.

Turn right and follow the Wandle Trail along the riverside, with alder trees lining the bank and sports fields on your left. Pass a skatepark, cross Kimber Road

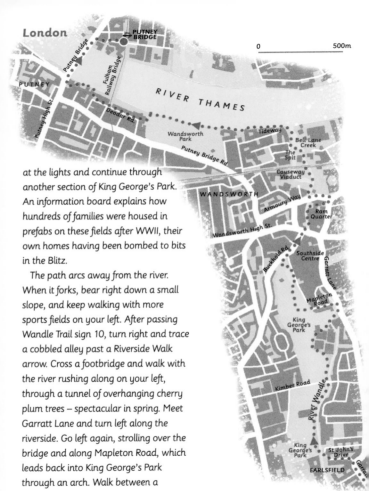

PUTNEY BRIDGE

PUTNEY

Putney Bridge

Fulham Railway Bridge

Putney High St.

Deodar Rd.

RIVER THAMES

0   500m

Wandsworth Park

Putney Bridge Rd.

Tideway

Bell Lane Creek

The Split

Causeway Viaduct

WANDSWORTH

Armoury Way

Ram Quarter

Wandsworth High St.

Buckhold Rd.

Southside Centre

Garratt Lane

Mapleton Road

King George's Park

River Wandle

Kimber Road

King George's Park

St John's Drive

EARLSFIELD

at the lights and continue through another section of King George's Park. An information board explains how hundreds of families were housed in prefabs on these fields after WWII, their own homes having been bombed to bits in the Blitz.

The path arcs away from the river. When it forks, bear right down a small slope, and keep walking with more sports fields on your left. After passing Wandle Trail sign 10, turn right and trace a cobbled alley past a Riverside Walk arrow. Cross a footbridge and walk with the river rushing along on your left, through a tunnel of overhanging cherry plum trees – spectacular in spring. Meet Garratt Lane and turn left along the riverside. Go left again, strolling over the bridge and along Mapleton Road, which leads back into King George's Park through an arch. Walk between a children's playground and ornamental

The River Wandle from Colliers Wood to the Thames

gardens, before turning right along a path beside tennis courts. Opposite a picnic area, go right to cross the pond via a pretty little stone bridge, then turn left. At the pond's end, where a large willow weeps into the water, leave the park and walk directly ahead to Buckhold Road. Cross at the lights and turn right to reach Wandsworth High Street, by the Southside Centre. Use the lights and go straight over. Continue towards the river, cross the footbridge and turn left along Barley Walk, with the water on your left. To the right is the Ram Quarter, historic home of Young's Ram Brewery, where beer has been made since the 16th century.

Follow a fingerpost right for Wandsworth Riverside Pier and walk along Chivers Passage. Go left along Ram Street to meet Armoury Way. Turn right for Wandsworth Town station (four minutes' walk) or continue towards the Thames by crossing Armoury Way at the lights and going left, following a Thames Cycle Route arrow.

Cross the bridge, then go right along The Causeway with the river on your right. Pass a weir and inlet, and continue under the Causeway Viaduct arches, past another weir, to a T-junction with the Thames Path. A right turn leads to Wandsworth and Battersea bridges, but this route turns left towards Wandsworth Park and Putney Bridge. First, though, explore The Spit – a tiny triangular causeway and nature reserve poking out into the river – to witness the Wandle flowing into the Thames. Return to the main path, cross a bridge, turn right and walk west along the riverside path through Wandsworth Park, passing Alan Thornhill's *Pygmalion*, part of the Putney Sculpture Trail, and umpteen London plane trees. Follow the path around the park's western corner, leaving the riverside briefly to turn right along Deodar Road. Go under Fulham Railway Bridge, dogleg around the Order of Malta building and continue along the Thames Path to Putney High Street. Turn right and cross Putney Bridge to the tube station.

Beckenham Place Park

Distance 3.5km **Time** 1 hour 30
Start Ravensbourne ⇥
Finish Beckenham Hill ⇥

Sprawling across almost 100 hectares, Beckenham Place Park is southeast London's largest green space, yet it remains one of its best-kept secrets – perhaps because it was only recently regenerated, re-opening in 2019 with land previously dominated by a golf course transformed into a freely accessible outdoor oasis with facilities that include a wild swimming and paddling lake, and a sensory garden.

This short point-to-point stroll explores a once-private estate and farm with a history dating back a millennia, mentioned in the Domesday Book. It's now a public park offering myriad wildlife encounters and a wealth of fascinating walking trails wending through ancient native woodland punctuated by exotic species introduced over the centuries by green-fingered former custodians.

Leave Ravensbourne railway station, carefully cross the road and scuttle left up Crab Hill road. After 50m, turn right through Crab Gate, following a Green Chain Walk (GCW) waymarker into the verdant embrace of Beckenham Place Park. Stroll along a broad unsealed track, passing purple-topped wooden posts, to a pebble-embedded area, where an information board explains how this exceptionally rare exposed section of a sedimentary rock layer, known as the Blackheath Beds, formed 55 million years ago when London was beneath the sea.

At a fingerpost, turn left, heading towards Foxgrove. Emerge by Crab Hill Field, a grassy expanse where crab apple trees once proliferated, which blooms with wildflowers in summer, attracting multitudes of butterflies and other pollinators. Turn right by an information board detailing how the meadow was used for military purposes during WWII, and descend along a briefly sealed track.

Meeting a crosspaths go left and then, at a triangular junction, keep bearing left, following Woodland Wander arrows.

177

BECKENHAM
HILL

SOUTHEND

Beckenham Hill Rd.

Mounded
Garden

Stableyards
café

Swimming
Lake

Wet
Woodland

Mansion
House

Beckenham
Place
Park

Ravensbourne River

Summerhouse
Hill Wood

Crab Hill
Field

Hayes Hill Rd.

RAVENSBOURNE

0   500m

At a fingerpost with arms pointing towards Foxgrove, Mansion House and Stableyards, ignore all these options and turn sharp right along a smaller path leading deep into Summerhouse Hill Wood, tracing Woodland Wander waymarkers as the path bends beneath the boughs of oak, sweet chestnut, holly, laurel and wild service trees. Continue past an open section, with a view left to the Stableyards, to meet a main track by an information board describing this ancient woodland's fauna and flora.

Turn left and walk along a sealed path, past cedar trees, to Beckenham Place Park Swimming Lake, a 285m-long purpose-built bathing and boating lake where lifeguards watch over wild swimmers and paddlers during daylight hours (pre-book sessions online) Leave the lake and ascend towards the Mansion House, Stableyards and Formal Gardens. Pass a squirrel statue and a gnarly 200-year-old mulberry tree, and continue past the Homestead entrance, following GCW and Capital Ring waymarkers to reach the house. Built in the 1760s by wealthy Quaker timber merchant John Cator, this Palladian mansion has been a family residence, school, sanatorium, wartime internment centre and golf clubhouse, but it's now used for community activities. There's also a basement bar and beer garden, ideal for sipping cold drinks on warm days, while enjoying sweeping views.

Loop the mansion, then go along the road briefly, before turning right into the walled Stableyards, where there's food and toilet facilities. Exit through a brick doorway left of the café, descend steps and walk straight across the gardens. Just before a children's play area, turn right and follow a path downhill towards the lake. Go through a metal gate to reach the shore and turn left, walking with the water on your right, busy with waterfowl ranging from Egyptian goose and Mandarin duck to little grebes, cormorants, coots, egrets, tufted ducks and moorhens. If you're lucky you might spot herons hunting or catch the iridescent flash of a passing kingfisher.

Continue around the lake to the Wet Woodland, part of the original Georgian-era lake, deliberately left unrestored to encourage wetland-loving trees (like willow and alder), birds (such as marsh and willow tits, siskin and redpoll), animals (frogs, toads and bats) and wildflowers, including marsh-marigold and meadowsweet. It's a fascinating and evolving environment to explore, but this walk leans left, following a fingerpost towards the Mounded Garden.

Pass the mound itself, a feature created with dirt discarded during the excavation of the swimming lake, or climb it to score views across the treetops, then continue to a T-junction. Go right, following a fingerpost towards a skatepark and BMX track. Cross a bridge over railway tracks, turn left by a purple-topped wooden post, descend steps and follow a path running alongside the railway line. Progress past a fingerpost to a sealed lane leading to Beckenham Hill Road. Turn left, cross at the lights and walk straight along an alley to Beckenham Hill Station.

179

29

Petts Wood and the River Cray

Distance 12.5km **Time** 4–5 hours
Start Chislehurst ≈
Finish Bexley ≈

This walk explores the secrets of Greater London's southeast corner via a section of the London Loop, trekking through the treescape of Hawkwood and Petts Wood to discover time-shifting pioneers and multi-storied historic houses, before following the curvaceous River Cray across parkland and wildflower-bejewelled meadows.

Leave Chislehurst station (close to the famous 'caves' created by 700 years of flint and chalk mining) and turn right into Station Approach. Cross Summer Hill via the footbridge and walk along Gosshill Road with the railway on your right. Continue through bollards and past a car-free section until you meet a gate on your left. Go through and follow fingerposts pointing towards Chislehurst Common. Just before a footbridge across Kyd Brook, turn right, pass the National Trust (NT) sign for

Hawkwood Estate and stroll along the path with the stream on your left.

Meadows open up on the right, dazzling with wildflowers in spring and summer. At a T-junction by a bridge, turn right and walk away from the brook. Pass another NT sign and follow the path as it bears left and runs parallel to the railway track. Go past a bridge over the railway (don't cross) and an NT sign for Petts Wood, and continue, wandering along a wooden boardwalk and crossing a footbridge over a stream.

As you enter the woods, the trail splays various ways. Stick to the main path, pass a wooden post and follow London Loop waymarkers up a gentle incline. At a fork just beyond some shallow wooden steps, go right and take the rutted path through oak, ash, holly, hazel and silver birch, before crossing a boardwalk and ascending slightly. The railway remains on your right, and occasionally the rumble of a train interrupts the serenity.

At a major T-junction, turn right very briefly, then follow a wide track left, walking gradually uphill, past trees marked with blue-and-white stripes (indicating a bridleway). Continue to a wooden post at a fork, then bear left, following London Loop waymarkers past chestnut trees and large oaks with bridleway markings. On the left, slightly off the path, is an NT memorial to Francis Joseph Frederick Edlmann, who saved these woods from development in 1927.

Continue along the main track with Edlmann Memorial Wood on your left and Willett Wood on the right, ascending a path fringed with ferns and sweet chestnut trees. At a wooden post,

leave the London Loop to turn right along the NT's Woodland Walk (waymarked with green footprints within arrows), leading to the Willett Sundial, which is set to GMT +1 and commemorates William Willett, a local builder who conceived the idea of moving clocks forward for summer while riding through Petts Wood one dark morning, and subsequently advocated vigorously for its implementation; sadly he died in 1915, a year before Daylight Savings began.

Walk past the sundial, leave the Woodland Walk and pass a bench,

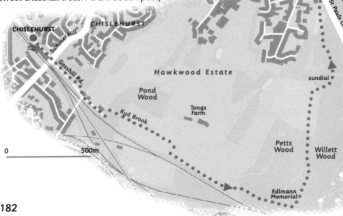

off and stroll along a gravel lane for 100m before turning right along a footpath, following London Loop arrows. After 100m turn left again, then at a T-junction go right. Pass a fingerpost and head towards the 'Moated Manor', tracing wooden posts with green claws. Go down steps by an enormous oak and keep gently descending past a tree-stump seat carved like a bear.

A London Loop waymarker on a wooden post sends you scooting past Scadbury Manor, a ruined moat-encircled mansion on a 13th-century estate, occupied for centuries by the wealthy Walsingham family (who counted Sir Francis Walsingham, known as Queen Elizabeth I's 'spymaster', among their ranks).

After this diversion, follow a fingerpost pointing to 'Acorn Trail Post 12'. When you meet a fence, turn left, continue to a crosspaths and fingerpost, then go right towards 'Little Wood'. Pass a green pond on your right, and keep going straight on, through a gate and along an undulating path beneath towering pines. Pass a fingerpost and continue until you meet the main road (A20).

then turn left along a bridleway (following trees daubed with blue-and-white paint). Go right at a large junction just before a Chislehurst Commons sign, leaving the bridleway and rejoining the London Loop. Pass a beautiful beech tree on your right, continue past a wooden post, ignore a path joining from the left and keep walking until you reach a road and a London Loop fingerpost.

Carefully cross and enter St Paul's Cray Common. Ignore small tracks spidering

Go through a metal gate, turn left and immediately left again, before ducking right through South Subway, passing beneath the road to the roundabout. Cross the bridge, turn right through another subway signed for Crittall's Corner and Swanley, then go left, following London Loop waymarkers and signs for Queen Mary's Hospital and Sidcup.

Bus 269 goes back to Chislehurst station from the first bus stop encountered after exiting the subway, if you've had enough. Otherwise, proceed along Frognal Avenue to Chislehurst Road, walk past Christ the King St Mary's sixth-form college (on the opposite side of the road), then follow a London Loop fingerpost pointing right, into Sidcup Place, going through railings and passing tennis courts on your left. Bear left to explore the walled community gardens, or visit The Star, a palatial pub. Continue with a ha-ha wall to your right, before following a fingerpost and London Loop way-markers leading right towards Foots Cray Meadows. Leave the sealed path and walk across the grass, passing a playground on your left and going through a gap in the trees, then continuing towards the bottom left corner of the lower field where a path leads through trees to a kissing gate.

Go through and follow the alleyway past a Scout hut and allotments. When the path forks, go right, passing through a gate, along a path, through another kissing gate and then turning left along the tarmac path. Go through

OLD BEXLEY

High St.

BEXLEY

cricket pitch

0   500m

Bexley Playing Field

play park

Woollett Hall Farm

Riverside Road

River Cray

Water Lane

North Cray Rd.

Five Arch Bridge

a gate, turn right along Suffolk Road, then left on Cray Road. Head straight over at the crossroads and ramble along Rectory Lane, past Footscray village war memorial and Hope School. Ignore the first path leading right, then just before the bend, turn right through a gate and trace Cray Riverway towards Old Bexley. Follow London Loop

waymarkers over pretty Pennyfarthing Bridge, crossing the River Cray into fantastic Foots Cray Meadows Nature Reserve, where a wealth of wildlife thrives on land once occupied by Foots Cray Place and North Cray Place Estates, both landscaped by Capability Brown in the 1780s. Turn left along the riverbank, where oak, ash and weeping willows shelter countless bird species, from kingfishers to treecreepers.

Pass fabulous Five Arch Bridge on your left, one of Capability Brown's surviving flourishes, and continue through the meadows. Ignore the first footbridge you pass, but cross over the river at the second one, before following the path to a road and turning right. At the end of the road a path leads across Bexley Playing Field, goes through a gate and passes an orchard and cricket pitch to arrive at Bexley Station.

30

The Ingrebourne Valley

Distance 8km **Time 3 hours**
Start Upminster Bridge ⊖
Finish Rainham ⇌

The Ingrebourne, one of London's most significant natural waterways, flows for 43km from its source in Navestock and South Weald, near Brentwood in Essex, to meet the mighty Thames in Rainham. This point-to-point adventure joins the river in Upminster to trace its final flourish through a huge 146-hectare nature reserve and explore Hornchurch Country Park, a former RAF base from where planes took off to defend London during both World Wars.

Along the route, pillboxes and gun emplacements remain in place as pertinent reminders of the horror of conflict, looking incongruous amid the green and serene surrounds of what has evolved to become a verdant ribbon-shaped retreat from the clamour of urban life.

Leave Upminster Bridge tube station and turn right on Upminster Road, passing under the railway bridge. Cross Norfolk Road and continue past The Windmill, a pub named after the real Upminster Windmill, which occupies a park further along the road (a bit beyond this route). Go over a bridge spanning the Ingrebourne River and cross Abraham Court, before turning right down Bridge Avenue. Just past a sign for 'Bridge Avenue nos 44-48a', turn right into Hornchurch Stadium. Pass the football club on your right, then turn left through the car park, going past a wide metal gate and entering a patchwork of fields and meadows collectively called Gaynes Parkway.

Stick to the sealed path, which soon sees you strolling beside the banks of the Ingrebourne River, with London Loop arrows also pointing the way. A stream comes in from the left and you pass a weir. As you wander, look out for little water voles darting around the riverside and nibbling on grass; although often mistaken for rats (a confusion not helped by Kenneth Grahame naming his water vole character 'Ratty' in *Wind in the*

Willows), these lovely little rodents are an essential part of the riparian ecosystem, and a joy to watch. Several picnic benches gaze across the water, and the riverbank and footpath are lined with ash, oak, crack willow and sycamore trees. Blackberries bulge among the bushes and stain the floor in summer.

The path elbows right, crosses a footbridge over the river and then turns left. Walk with the water on your left until the route bears right and crosses Hacton Lane at the lights. Continue straight, into Hacton Park, following London Loop and Havering Greenways waymarkers. Pass to the left of a children's playground and continue along the sealed path through the pleasant park, passing several epic oaks. Alternatively, walk across the grass to trace the Ingrebourne's curves and get closer to the river. Several sections feature little steps leading down to the water, which is fringed with wildflowers in summer, including pink Himalayan balsam, hairy willowherb, creeping thistle and purple loosestrife.

Upminster Rd.

UPMINSTER BRIDGE

Hornchurch Stadium

Bridge Av

HORNCHURCH

Gaynes Parkway

Hacton Lane

Hacton Park

Ingrebourne Valley Nature Reserve

INGREBOURNE VALLEY

Ingrebourne River

Suttons Lane

Discovery Centre (café)

Hornchurch Country Park

0   500m

To Rainham

Pass a metal fence, proceed into other part of the park and keep going st a sign for Ingrebourne Valley Local ature Reserve, walking through box der and hawthorn trees. A fingerpost ints left across a wooden bridge for acton Lane and right to indicate an ternative route, but keep going straight th the river on your left (albeit mostly dden behind oak trees, reeds and thick liage). The waterway reappears in veral spots, though, and benches offer pportunities for rest and contemplation mid the quietude.

Cross a little wooden bridge spanning incoming stream (or go through the etal gate beside it) and ascend a small cline. Pass another children's ayground and note the Royal Air Force emorial on your left. Also here, on the ft, is the Essex Wildlife Trust's grebourne Nature Discovery Centre, pen daily 10am–4pm (longer in ummer), where you'll find a café, toilet cilities, plenty of picnic benches and ts of fascinating information about the arshland and reedbeds of the River grebourne Valley, which the building ramatically overlooks.

Take the dirt path here for a wilder experience as the valley drops away to your left, but do explore sections of the 'Peri Track' which once formed the tarmac perimeter around the grass runways where rickety-looking biplanes (including the famous Sopwith Camel) took off during WWI to repel Zeppelin raids, and Spitfires were scrambled to engage Luftwaffe bombers as they approached London during WWII.

When the track splits by some outdoor gym equipment and benches, take the left fork for 'Albyns farm and lake' (alternatively, you can go right if you really want to avoid the hill). To your left lie Ingrebourne Marshes, a safe haven for wildlife, including birds such as bittern, and sedge and willow warblers. Kestrels and marsh harriers often hover overhead, as kingfishers dart past in a barely perceivable flash of iridescence. House martins, hobby, swallows and swifts are seasonal visitors, while little egret, ringed plover and lapwing are resident all year here. Dragonflies and butterflies are present for the warmer months, and if you're really lucky you may even spot a stoat.

Pass a fingerpost for Berwick Wood to the left, but continue straight towards the farm and lake. You're well within the grounds of Hornchurch Country Park now, a historic place inextricably entwined with the World Wars. While ascending a slight rise you pass a control tower post, and when you descend the other side

you will see, on your left, a type 22 WWII pillbox. These structures were designed to provide a last line of defence if enemy forces were approaching central London. Continue past a Tett Turret (a tiny claustrophobia-inducing concrete-lined hole in the ground, big enough for just one gunman) and another pillbox on your left, before proceeding up a little incline and passing another pillbox on the right which has a more complex design and a hidden entrance, and was possibly intended for use as the battle HQ.

Reach Tit Lake and walk left along the bank, with the water on your right. Look and listen out for pond life, which includes common frogs and toads, as well as a multitude of waterfowl. Follow he sealed path as it turns right up to Albyns Farm. Walk around a large metal gate, and past the impressive farmhouse, then head left through another metal gate, following the fingerpost for Ingrebourne Hill. Stroll with a lovely wide meadow on your left, fringed with wildflowers including mallow, yarrow and ragwort in summer.

Keep tracing the sealed track, turning right through a gate and then going immediately left along a gravel path with a hedge on your left, full of rosehip and wild cherry. Climb the hill and pass some cycling tracks, part of the Ingrebourne Hill Bike Park's network of trails. Keep going straight along the main trail, as the bike tracks cross your path again.

When the path forks, turn left. Pass the trailhead of the bike path network and keep going straight, past a car parking area. When you reach some metal gates, turn right and emerge on busy Rainham Road. Turn left and walk past The Albion pub into historic Rainham, where evidence of human habitation stretches way beyond the Roman era, and finds have included the 'Havering hoard', a haul of Bronze Age bracelets, swords and axes.

Stay on the left side of the road. At a large roundabout, cross at the lights to go straight ahead, following London Loop pointers. Cross Red Bridge over the Ingrebourne River. A creek-side path leads left here, if you want to explore Rainham itself. Otherwise, carry on straight, crossing the small road and following signage for the railway station. Pass a supermarket and continue straight ahead at the roundabout, walking along Bridge Road, past the Georgian mansion Rainham Hall (maintained by the National Trust, and used as Ebenezer Scrooge's house in the 2019 BBC production of Dickens' *A Christmas Carol*) and the library. Turn right on Old Station Lane, then left on Celtic Farm Road, which leads to the station.

Index